There Is No Night

For Martin & Hilary
with love
from

John

There Is No Night
New and Selected Poems

John Purser

WITH THREE POEMS BY
SEAN PURSER

and an Introduction
by Alan Riach

Kennedy & Boyd

Kennedy & Boyd
an imprint of
Zeticula Ltd
The Roan
Kilkerran
KA19 8LS
Scotland.

http://www.kennedyandboyd.co.uk
admin@kennedyandboyd.co.uk

First published in 2014
Copyright © John Purser 2014

Introduction Copyright © Alan Riach 2014
Cover Design Copyright © Seán Purser 2014

ISBN 978-1-84921-144-4

For my sister Geraldine

Contents

Preface xiii
Acknowledgements xvii
Introduction xix

In the Manuscript Room of the Library 1
The Laughter of the Sea (from *Six Sea Poems* by Sean Purser) 2

Crofting Poems 3
Wooden Tongue 5
A Share of the Wind 6
White Rainbow 7
Sore Udder in Summer 8
Cleaning the Net 10
Archie 12
Mastitis 14
Aristocracy 15
The Incorruptible Crofter 16
Arthritis 17
November from the Clach Rathad 18
Near Eniskillen 19
Grass Snake 20
Glen Scaladal 21
Croftwork 22

The Counting Stick 25
The Counting Stick 27

Songs of Occupation   31
    The Organist Confesses to His Mirror   33
    Lines for My Quern   34
    Lines for My Sundial   35
    For the Old Men of the Shells   36
    For the Old Women of the Shells   37
    The Piano Tuner   38
    On the Arklow Lightship   39
    At the Conference   40
    Quarry   41
    In Antalya   42
    Chocolate   43

Amoretti   45
    I   47
    II   48
    III   49
    IV   50
    V   51
    VI   52
    VII   53
    VIII   54
    IX   55
    X   56
    XI   57
    XII   58
    XIII   59
    XIV   60
    XV   61
    XVI   62
    XVII   63
    XVIII   64
    XIX   65
    XX   66
    XXI   67
    XXII   68
    XXIII   69

Stornelli   71
    Three Stornelli   73
    Four Stornelli   74
    Three Echo Stornelli   75

Cherry-Tree Poems   77
    I   79
    III   80
    VII   81
    VIII   82
    IX   83
    X   84

New World Poems   85
    Nashawena   87
    Naushon   88
    Nashawena Shoreline   89
    Cape Cod Clearing   90
    Duck Pond   91
    At the Red House   92
    Penikese   93
    On South Bluffs Road   94
    Towards the Western Bluffs   95
    At the Top of the Island   96

Love Poems   97
    Lines for a Wedding Pledge, for Marcus and Julie Longmuir   99
    No Nightfall in June   100
    On the Hill Brow   101
    Valentine   102
    After-Dinner Grace in Monometers, For Two Only 103
    Out of Season   106
    Valentine   107

Birthday Poems   109
    For Kirsten MacLeod on Her Fourteenth Birthday 111
    For Meg Bateman on the Occasion of her Fiftieth Birthday 112
    For Ivan Mavor   114

Northern Latitudes   115
    Scotland's Thistle   117
    At the Giants' Graves   118
    In Winter   119
    Northern Latitudes   120
    Iceland Seen from Skye   121

Six Composers   125
    Erik Chisholm   127
    Alexander Campbell MacKenzie   129
    Hamish MacCunn   130
    Michael Marra   132
    William Kinloch   133
    John Blackwood McEwen   136

Family Poems   137
    Family   139
    Sarah   140
    Interior   141
    Pattern of Waves   142
    Bathing (from *Six Sea Poems* by Sean Purser) 143
    Farmer   144
    Bray Head   145
    Domestic Interior   146
    For my Daughter in Black   147
    For my Son who Would Wear Motley   148
    For Judith Caughie   149
    For Judith and Simon Sweeney 15.10.11   150
    For my Grandson Thomas Sean Gormley   151
    And for His Mother, my Daughter Sarah   152
    For Paul Gormley   153

Bird Poems   155
    Phalacrocorax Aristotelis (The Shag, or Skart) 156
    Adolescent   157
    Champion   158
    Snow Bunting   160
    The Swift   161
    A Message to Hirini Melbourne   162
    Skylark   164
    It is Dusk   165

Poems and Dialogues Concerning Natural Religion   167
    Jehovah's Witness on Skye   169
    Columba to God   172
    Columba to King David   173
    Columba and Saint Finnian   174
    Saint Brigid to Christ   175
    Ranging   176
    The Translator Confesses to the Book of Books   177
    Homage to David Hume   178
    One Irishman to Another   179
    The View from October Hills   180
    The Hot Coal of Truth   182
    The Poet to Plato   183
    Ballade for the Duke of Orléans   184
    Mummified Nun   185
    Léborcham to Conchobar   186
    Gráinne to Diarmait   187
    Botticelli to Venus   188
    The Deeps (from *Six Sea Poems* by Sean Purser)   189

Three Stone Boats   191
    For Will MacLean   193
    For Bonnie Rideout   194
    For Barbara Purser   195

Dedicatory Poems   197
    For Sorley MacLean   198
    To His Family in Memory of William Angel   199
    For Professor Doctor Ellen Hickmann   200
    For Maria Papageorgiou   201
    For Martin Dalby   202
    For Franco Staffa   203
    Homage to Jack Yeats   204
    In Memory of Mainie Jellett   206
    A City Herald   207
    For Katherine and Elliot Forbes on Their Final Move
     to the Banks of The Charles River   208
    For Hinewirangi Kohu   209
    For Sir Iain Noble, 8.1.2010   210

Poets in Kelvingrove Art Gallery 212
Old Photograph 213

To Be Sung In Orbit 214

To the Library of Scottish Poetry 215

Preface

I am the son of a poet. My father published three books with the Fortune Press. We used to write each other poems when I was a little boy in a preparatory school; sometimes a poem a week, so poetry was always a natural thing to me, part of letter-writing and simply another way of responding to the world.

Sometimes I write in strict forms, sometimes in free verse: but at all times I take delight in assonance and alliteration and an underlying sense of pulse. Beauty of sound is important to me, and I acquired that love not only because I am a musician, but because much of my early knowledge of poetry was of Irish verse. I love words – their taste, texture and sound – but of course above all, I care for their meaning. On the other hand, I make very little use of simile or metaphor. I like to describe things as they are and on their own terms. For similar reasons, I prefer to keep some sense of coherent grammatical structure alive in my work, in the interests of clarity – but I hope I have found room too for mystery, and for thoughts which are not susceptible to easy analysis.

Most of my poems are responses to direct personal experience and, in that sense, they are occasional. In the case of the Crofting Poems, it was physical events – often necessities – which made me stop and think or, when there was no time to stop and think, reflect upon them later. I've been a crofter on the Isle of Skye for seventeen years now, and involved in farming and crofting for much of my life. There may not be much room for sentiment in crofting, but regular contact with other species soon teaches one to respect their place in the world, and to recognise that we humans are not as separated from them as we might like to suppose. The Crofting, Cherry-Tree and Bird Poems sections may focus on such thoughts, but almost the entire collection draws on the natural environment, including the New World Poems, and Northern Latitudes.

Amongst the Amoretti – a group of love poems for my wife, Barbara – there are many which were prompted by our shared experience as crofters. The title of this sequence is filched from Spenser. It is supposed to mean "little love letters", but it is bad Italian. What matters to me is that Spenser, almost alone amongst writers of love sonnets, expresses joy and satisfaction rather than misery and resentment. Not all the poems are in sonnet form and, in those which are, I have occasionally allowed extra syllables in the final line, as did Sidney.

I enjoy the challenges of strict poetic form, and the collection includes many sonnets. There are two poems in iambic monometers, in which every second syllable must rhyme, and there is also a group of Stornelli. This Italian verse form was traditionally improvised, despite its strict requirements. I came across it when staying in a village which had been on the German side of the Gothic line in the Second World War. The villagers used improvised stornelli, which they chanted or sang in the vineyards and chestnut woods, to pass information across the valley about the movement of German patrols. Occasional verses indeed.

It seems to me to be an important part of the social function of a poet to meet the needs of occasions. The group of Birthday Poems, and a number of the Family and Dedicatory Poems, were obviously composed for specific events, including births, birthdays, marriages and deaths. I have also written many others not included here, a good few of them humorous.

There is a substantial section of Poems and Dialogues Concerning Natural Religion. The title of this group is taken from David Hume, in homage to whom one of the poems was written. Some of them are philosophical, others are responses to mythology. The Counting Stick might have found a place in that group, but it is long enough to stand on its own. It was inspired by a young shepherd resting with his flock high in the hills of Provence. He was passing the time marking a stick with a penknife, in surroundings little altered in a thousand years.

My initial training was as a musician – specifically as a composer. In later life I had the opportunity to broadcast and publish a substantial body of work about Scotland's Music. This included researching and reviving the works of many neglected Scottish composers. Six of them feature in a section·of their own. They are discursive poems – conversations almost, with people I never really knew except through their music.

I owe a debt of gratitude to many fellow poets over several decades. Stewart Conn was the first to encourage me as a poet, and broadcast a number of my poems, including a radio play, *Papageno*, which was centred on my poetic response to events in a northern Italian village. Liz Lochhead encouraged me to contact my first publisher – Jim Green of Aquila Press, and Jim published my three earlier collections – *The Counting Stick*, *A Share of the Wind*, and *Amoretti*. William Turner put me through a brief but strict apprenticeship, and, over the years, Stewart and Judy Conn and Alan Riach in particular, have read and suggested revisions for much of my work, and rescued me from all sorts of stupidities and poverties of expression: and Meg Bateman has cast a genial and critical eye over some of my more recent work.

My wife, Barbara, has been a most helpful critic and supporter, and above all, she has been the inspiration for many of the poems. She is the recipient of the third of three stone boat poems. I made these boats almost entirely out of marble. They are very small and, because they might seem rather foolish, I accompanied each one with an explanatory poem – but of course the boats, just like the poems which follow, can also speak for themselves.

Acknowledgements

Many of these poems were published previously, either in *The Counting Stick*, *A Share of the Wind*, and *Amoretti*, published by Aquila Press, or in anthologies and magazines. These latter are listed below in the order in which they re-appear in this book, though often with revisions. My thanks to their editors for their support over the decades. 'Sore Udder In Summer' (*Scottish Poetry* 9, 1976 as 'Milking'); 'Cleaning the Net' (*Lines Review*, 1995); 'Glen Scaladal' (*Chapman* 82, 1995); 'Croftwork' (*The Dark Horse*, Summer 2007); 'The Organist Confesses To His Mirror' (*Words* 3, 1977 and *The Edinburgh Book of Twentieth-Century Scottish Poetry*, 2005); 'Lines For My Quern' - Worked by a Man and Worked by a Woman' (*Words* 3, 1977); 'Lines For My Sundial - At Night and At Noon' (Words 3, 1977); 'The Piano Tuner' (*Scottish Poetry* 8, 1975); 'In Antalya' (*Lion's Milk / Aslan Sütü*, 2012); 'Amoretti XIII' (*100 Favourite Scottish Love Poems*, 2008); 'Amoretti XIV' (*Chapman* 82, 1995); 'Amoretti XV' (*Chapman* 82, 1995); 'Amoretti XVII' (*Chapman* 108, 2006); 'Amoretti XVIII' (*McCarapace, Carapace* No 18 c.1997); 'Amoretti XX' (*Chapman* 108, 2006); 'Cherry-Tree Poems' (I *Scottish Poetry* 7, 1974, I *Trees* 1975, I *Touch Wood*, 1990); 'No Nightfall in June' (*The Edinburgh Book of Twentieth-Century Scottish Poetry*, 2005); 'Valentine' (*Carapace* 52, 2005); 'Scotland's Thistle' (*Scotia Nova*, 2014); 'In Winter' (*100 Favourite Scottish Poems to be Read Aloud*, 2007); 'Northern Latitudes' (*Scotlands*, 2004); 'Bray Head' (*Lines Review*, 1995); 'For my Daughter in Black' (*Chapman* 82, 1995); 'For my Son who Would Wear Motley' (*Chapman* 82, 1995); 'For My Grandson Thomas Gormley' (*Carapace* 57, 2006); 'And For His Mother, My Daughter Sarah' (*Carapace* 57, 2006); 'For Paul Gormley' (*Carapace* 57, 2006); 'Adolescent' ('Bird Without Song' in *A Nest of Singing Birds*, 1995); 'Champion' (*A Nest of Singing Birds*, 1995); 'The Swift' (*Birds*

1970s); 'Skylark' (*Carapace* 46, 2004); 'Jehovah's Witness on Skye' (*The Dark Horse* No 3, 1996); 'Columba To God' (*Chapman* 108, 2006 and *100 Favourite Scottish Poems*, 2006); 'Columba To King David' (*Chapman* 108, 2006); 'Brigid To Chris' (*Skinklin Star* Broadsheet, Issue Three, c.1997); 'The Translator Confesses To The Book Of Books' (Ó Snodaigh (Trans.) *Cumha agus Cumann*, Dublin 1985, 1987); 'Mummified Nun' (*Scottish Poetry* 8, 1975); 'Sir Alexander Campbell MacKenzie' (*The Dark Horse* 25, 2010); 'Erik Chisholm' (CD liner notes *Erik Chisholm Piano Music* Volume 7, Dunelm Records); 'Michael Marra' (*Scotia Nova*, 2014); 'For Martin Dalby' (published at BASCA 24th Gold Badge Awards 1998); 'Homage to Jack Yeats' (*Chapman* 82, 1995); 'A Message To Hirini Melbourne' (*Carapace* 51, 2004 and *Flute Focus* 4, 2005); 'A City Herald' (*Chapman* 108, 2006); 'For Will MacLean' (*The Dark Horse* 30 Spring/ Summer 2013).

Introduction

Alan Riach

The bowsprit, the arrow, the longing, the lunging heart –
the flight to a target whose aim we'll never know,
vain search for one island that heals with its harbor
and a guiltless horizon, where the almond's shadow
doesn't injure the sand. There are so many islands!
As many islands as the stars at night
on the branched tree from which meteors are shaken
like falling fruit around the schooner *Flight*.

from 'The Schooner *Flight*' (*The Star-Apple Kingdom*, 1980)

Derek Walcott, the Nobel Laureate of St Lucia, in the Caribbean, invites us to consider the archipelagos of islands, communities of different identity, that are, inescapably, the world from which he arose.

Equally various, and inescapable, the world John Purser makes for us in his poems, as in his music and his scholarship, is archipelagic, characterised by diversity and depths, bright sunlit perceptions and profundities of insight into the nature of the earth itself, and as far out as the music of the spheres permits us, granting self-awareness of, and exploring, not only knowledge, but intuitive awareness.

In his 'Author's Preface' to this book, he says that poetry is a 'natural thing', simply 'another way of responding to the world', implicitly along with music, painting, sculpture, the documentation of knowledge, shaping the world around you in whatever capacity you have, interpreting the world and representing it.

This might seem wishful, arbitrary or idealistic, except that Purser knows deeply that strict forms in poetry have their own profound purpose, and that if free verse might do its job without regular metre or rhyme, nevertheless anything that is, truly, poetry, always possesses 'an underlying sense of pulse'.

In John Purser's poems, there is relatively little in the way of metaphor: things are what they are, 'things as they are', yet always, everywhere, never forgotten, never neglected, is the sense that things are transformed through art, or as Wallace Stevens most memorably said:

> The man bent over his guitar,
> A shearsman of sorts. The day was green.
>
> They said, 'You have a blue guitar,
> You do not play things as they are.'
>
> The man replied, 'Things as they are
> Are changed upon the blue guitar.'
>
> And they said then, 'But play, you must,
> A tune beyond us, yet ourselves,
>
> A tune upon the blue guitar
> Of things exactly as they are.'

from *The Man with the Blue Guitar* (1937)

So all things work in metaphor, connectedness, the transport of language. I once said to John that I thought metaphor was wonderful, a great virtue human beings have and language gives us, and he expressed impatience with me: reality is the important thing – do not be distracted. Both of us were right, and wrong. Metaphor is what we do, as poets, artists, composers, and reality is not separate from this, but neither is art substitute for fact, or better, action. Food is never substitute for incident. Reality must never be neglected. And that is in the simplest terms: birth and growth and procreation, ageing, death, community and social, human, language and relation, care, love. What you learn from others, and what you learn from other living things –

other species, other life-forms, other people in the languages they live in – these are not things to be reduced to formulae or cliché, machinery or mechanical numbers.

Hugh MacDiarmid once wrote, in the middle of his enormous poem, *In Memoriam James Joyce* (1955): 'And all this here, everything I write, of course, / Is an extended metaphor for something I never mention.'

And of course, he never mentions it.

John Purser's poems are a vast and wonderful terrain of things not only mentioned but encountered, crossed and tenderly, touched, places and people, ideas and themes, emphatically demanding we prioritise, should pay attention to, should know and therefore act upon, the things that matter most. There is, time and again, the mysterious, but there is also the practical. Purser works as a crofter, he is literally in 'regular contact with other species' and this, in his poems, teaches us, as it has taught him, 'respect for their place in the world' and our place in our own, and where they overlap. The singular achievement of his poems is the delivery of this.

There are, as one might hope for and expect, many occasional poems: love poems, birthday poems, poems for festive events, dialogues, conversations with Scottish composers of older generations. And every one of these is worth a reader's close attention, for all sorts of reasons. The skill of composition in each one of them, the humanity engaged in their motivation as equally displayed in their delivery, the discrimination of their utterance, the joy in them.

Let's rehearse some of their virtues.

All great works of art get better, the more you know them. The more you read them, the deeper they become, the more they tell you things you had not fully known before. John Purser's poems are not the product of fashion or form, forged in the currency of critical discourse. They are made from his own life and training, in art, music and literary sense, and knowledge of and love of the world beyond art's mediation.

What are they, then?

The prelude is his father, Sean Purser, whose poems, 'The Laughter of the Sea', 'Bathing' and 'The Deeps' are reproduced here for two reasons. Their integrity and worth are self-evident, but the themes that arise there carry forward into John's work so clearly that it would be negligent not to acknowledge them, and let them speak for themselves. A full collection of Sean Purser's poems would be a good thing, both for the poems themselves and for the historical era they recollect, its priorities and preferences, virtues and thrills. But Sean's poems are also an acknowledgement of John's history. He is not an isolated poet, although his first-person singular is often just only and simply himself; he is, rather, a poet among company – like Burns, for example – always in dialogue with others, always asking questions or responding to, others. He is – and his poetry is – companionable, by definition. Not an isolato, then, but a man whose loneliness at times is revealed to us, to learn from. He is an antidote to celebrity culture because he is the singular person who is not to be celebrated as heroic or unique (although of course he is both) but to be worked with, constantly directing us to the authority of the community of us all. We participate in these poems, we are not simply readers of them – or else, what value do we have?

In that spirit, there are, I think, seven major themes in the collection as a whole that engage in different kinds of participation: they are those of **the archive**, the inherited history of past culture and its present applications; then there is the relationship between what we might call **inside and outside**, crudely put, interiors, indoor worlds, and the world beyond the self, beyond whatever securities we might have or make for ourselves; there is the theme of **origin**, in nature, wherever we come from, whatever we originate in, out of, something distinctive whose traces we carry forever; and there is **love**, in various forms, a continuing pulse, a ground base of sustaining understanding, something principled but not inflexible, strong but not invulnerable; there is the matter of **geography**, in different senses, the exploration of physical space, different countries or inter-continental locations, co-ordinate points, various parts of the earth; and there is his favoured, returned-to location, **the north**, as a direction and latitude, a broad but sharply drawn, inhabited space, different from others; and finally, not perhaps a theme so much as a form, that of implied or actual **dialogues**, the most obvious design for participatory poems, not theatrical drama but carefully constructed one-sided participations in conversations with other people, characters, creatures, living things who answer back, mostly implicitly, but sometimes in memorable words of their own, through voices that belong, not to personae, but to themselves.

1.

The book begins and ends in The Library. First, we are with the manuscripts, invited to trace antique connections of physicality, in human and non-human forms of life. In this increasingly digitised, mechanised age, this first principle marks what human beings do in the bodily act of inscription, writing as something arising from connections between vegetation, literally, the trees that go to papyrus, and the muscle, hand and eye of the writer, where ink – of whatever physical derivation (and there are many, including the blood in veins and arteries) – makes patterns through which meaning and music may be transmitted, with greater or less accuracy. The purpose is not to romanticise but rather to indicate 'the deep concentric memory / in the tree.' So the singular tree becomes a metaphor encompassing plurality, all the different ways of telling, all the different stories to be told.

At the end of the book, we are specifically approaching the Scottish Poetry Library, one of the most glorious establishments in modern Scotland's cultural history, founded by Tessa Ransford in 1984, a treasure in the capital's Royal Mile, where Purser's words may be seen on the corner of the building, crossing round at the line-break, from the Canongate into Crichton's Close. The abstract words – nation, poetry, and the bright image, 'forged in the hearth', combine in appropriate consequence, an optimistic promise of political, as well as literary, regeneration.

Beginning with metaphor, ending with actuality, the libraries that start and end the book suggest Walter Benjamin's wonderful essay, 'Unpacking My Library' (1931), collected in *Illuminations* (1970), translated by Harry Zohn. In the essay, the books are not yet on the shelves, and we join the author in their company in the disorder of opened crates, seeing them in daylight again after years of darkness. Likewise, we will see John Purser's poems in this collection in the light of a new day, collected and ordered into a comprehensive achievement as singular and impressive as any in the firmament. And as with Benjamin, at the end of his essay, Purser himself will disappear inside his library, 'as is only fitting'. But before we get there, there is a very big world to roam around in, explore and savour, and we will be in the company of one of the best guides there is.

2.

Perhaps the furthest we may travel keeps us in mind of the relationship between what's indoors and what's outdoors, or inside, in the most intimate senses, and what's so far beyond us we might not have thought how closely it is relevant, not only to our intellectual apprehension but also to our physical being.

In 'At the conference' (from the section entitled 'Songs of Occupation'), we are among scholars, studying words, on handouts on desks, with a thirst for knowledge and an atmosphere that 'dries the brain'. Yet the dry lips give pleasure to the tongue's moistening, and the taste left behind is savoured carefully and communally, a happy consecration. The physical intimacy and intellectual comprehension are mutual and nourishing.

A page or two later, there is 'In Antalya'. When I first read this poem, I was sceptical of John's proposition, and told him so. The idea that an anonymous old singer in southwestern Turkey might be giving voice to something 'older than geology' struck me as romantic hyperbole. But it is not, and John corrected me at once, and not for the first time. A song beyond memory, older than religions, older than humanity, older than cellular life or the deepest deep time of geology, is inherent to the universe we are given to inhabit. This is what was once familiarly called 'the music of the spheres'. Constellations, galaxies, forms through millennia, move in this music. There is no silence, in the end, only the movement of the song. What John describes in this unsought-for encounter is a serendipitous discovery, its meaning unwilled, unforced, native to matter itself. What connects us in every form of our sophistications should never completely ignore the vital context this gives us. And of course, we should never forget it.

The idea returns in the penultimate poem of the collection, 'To be sung in orbit', this time with personal and indeed romantic gestures and rhetorical questions. The imagery is precise: 'the slip of water on glass / or of threads spinning round / the spinner earth'. But everything in this poem has been earned, and it would simply be mean-spirited to deny the affirmation commanded by the asking of whether the poet should seek to defy accepted judgements, or spin songs in a lullaby mode. And the words in the poem themselves suggest more than one thing. Cocoons might bring comfort; they also precede and are part of the risk of transformation. Half-sleeping is also half-awake. Songs that pass beyond all hearing may always be somewhere, in orbit.

3.

But all things have origin. Beginnings are important. Where we start from is what gives us the respect we need. For Purser, this is measured most accurately through knowledge and experience of the work of the croft, and the natural world. The earth and the sea, farming and fishing, give us the sustenance required. Or rather, we work to gain our sustenance from them. Nothing is given without such work.

Here indeed there is a primary reality that spares no time for metaphor or simile, artistic elaborations and associations of perception. They will come and are never entirely absent, but the necessary facts are economic, reality, food, shelter, procreation, living together, communities of social politics that mean that people live in a cradle-balance with animals, other species, natural geography, earth and sea, the whole, complex ecologies of working economies.

These are not the sentimental indulgences of the ignorant visitor or happily tripping tourist, no matter how well-intentioned they might be. They are, rather, reports and mediations between the work of making a living as a crofter and the community of readers to whom the poems are addressed. There is of course an overlap between these two areas of work – crofting and reading – but the former, while it may be enjoyable and satisfying, is often much harder work than anything that might be called 'leisure' activity – while the latter *demands* leisure, and the choice made to occupy that leisure with work of a different kind. Purser's poems connect these two kinds of work without belittling, simplifying or sentimentalising either. This is a rare virtue in itself. Wordsworth, looking at a solitary reaper in a field, is on a walking tour. That solitary reaper is working in a different, but not completely unconnected, way. Both have their songs. Purser's representations of origins, in nature, are tougher than Wordsworth or any of the Romantics. There is death and unrecovering disability here, and there is elation, the sunshine of bright vision. But as with the great Gaelic poems, especially of the latter half of the 18th century, there is vital relation and connection between the earth and the sublime.

'The Counting Stick' is one of the most remarkable poems of this kind, and one of the finest 'nature' poems ever written. Sheep are recorded passing into a pen, the shepherd marking and recording them on his stick in a sequence of patterned marks: rings and diamonds. Hoggets, tups, ewes, the living animals pass the enumerating man, whose school-learning has only partly equipped him for the experience his life has to deal with. Equally, cutting through rock in the quarry, he measures earth in 'centuries / of sediments', thereby making 'fossils of his kind.' Time is itself the subject of the poem, ultimately, and how to measure it in value. That value will be obvious in economic terms, and these are never to be denied; but it is much more than numbers. Or rather, numbers help us understand what more there is in economics, as in music. 'Wooden Tongue' records the necessary killing of a cow, the comfort in seeing the first steps of a new calf, and the inarticulate sympathy and understanding that people share with animals. The detail of 'spades' that dig up 'the bluebell bulbs' to bury 'the bloated frame' is so vivid and tough, its authority is undeniable. We could not look away, and must not deny what necessity is, and the choices we must make to be responsible to it.

In 'A Share of the Wind', the human work done to assist in the birthing of a calf – bringing the creature into life with transmission of breath from mouth to mouth – is completed by the mother cow moving in, to lick and tear and nudge and massage him into life, leaving the instinct and gift of survival shared, as mortality is, though not, perhaps, the questioning foreknowledge of it. 'Poor cow' is literal in the poem whose title is brazen in its representation of the banality of utter pain, 'Sore Udder in Summer': an unsettling, discomforting, carefully and artfully constructed poem, whose two-word lines work their way down the page like chalk screeching on a blackboard, giving all the swollen sense of agony to the empty paper around. 'I grip / my hate' stands as a statement not only of opposition but also of recognition, resistant, intensely defiant, but accepting the inevitable too. And in 'White Rainbow' and 'Cleaning the Net', the complementary work of the fisherman balances that of the crofter. Again, the practicalities and hard facts are caught in the depictions, while the lyrical lightness of touch gives a terrific presence of sensual experience:

> There is a madness in it all
> the boat's slow dance
>
> the fish scales glittering
> on our coats...

And the net brought up from the sea to dry, draped on a pole, for the little crabs to be crushed and discarded with the clinging seaweed and jellyfish tentacles: 'utterly opposed / to the immaculate' but possessed of, possessing, in Purser's phrase, something 'brute sensitive' in all that remains, 'tangled widdershins'.

No poetry, except arguably that of John Clare, is as attentive to the reality of nature. Clare is selfless in his descriptions, where by contrast Burns is always in negotiation with nature and his person is present; Purser is in the company of both these two great nature poets, and he is between them, both present and selfless, in his recording of fact, and intervention in reality. The poems show this, again and again.

This context of sensitivity and necessity pervades the poems 'Croftwork', with its shocking immediacy in the description of shooting a calf 'Good gun the merciful', and 'Lines for My Quern', with its distinctions noted, whether the quern is 'Worked by a Man' or 'Worked by a Woman'. The extreme conservatism of the gender-roles depicted in these poems is not simply a matter of social organisation or chosen structuring, but rather a courageous coming-to-terms with inescapable facts of elemental reality. Working the quern – making bread, creating nourishment from seed, flour, 'grains of sun', 'meal' – are different in the physical worlds of women and men, and the relation described here arises from respect and understanding, rather than chosen priorities of dominance and power. The power is in nature, which is fearfully, but nurturingly, comprehensive. The same matter arises in 'For the Old Men of the Shells' and 'For the Old Women of the Shells': imagery of scallop shells as whisky cups or spoons to skim cream from shallow bowls counterpoints, complements and holds men and women in balance: 'love's badge of pilgrimage' is possessed by both, and both, like all memories, become 'impotent in the face of time'.

But more than time can bring on impotence. Powerlessness can be imposed, power taken away by force, and in the evocation of the clearances in 'Glen Scaladal', it is the barrenness that remains in the unspoken, because depopulated, terrain, that prompts 'griefs / frowning and weeping'. Typically, the words note the responses of anger and sorrow, neither lingering nor self-indulgently lamenting. Nature offers up its own imagery of devastation: the iris is 'stately and fine' but a 'spent ewe' has been devoured by foxes and crows, the lamb's head in its torn womb eyeless. The understatement is chilling: 'There are no children here' and no 'warm comfort of humanity.' This is a lyrical, autobiographical poem in which the poet encounters real things, but it is also an exposition of Scottish history, and even more, it is a political indictment of bad government and evil power in any era, including here and now.

Yet also within the scope of Purser's vision, just as one is tender to the 'wrinkled skin and knotted hand' in 'For the Old Women of the Shells', there is the sheer domestic pleasure of surrender to the night-time 'Chocolate' (or rather, as it used to be, 'cocoa'): powder, warm milk, sugar, a making of intimate, renewing nourishment that takes us into the delectable communion between 'you / and the mug and the cocoa' and gets down to the last 'dark circle round the base' inside the mug, scooped up with the spoon, 'that sweet and bitter taste' we won't forget, before night sets in.

Such matters of origin in nature and communion have their various manifestations, and what is sustained in more than one series of poems collected here is their centre: love.

4.

The love poems in this collection are perhaps its most startling accomplishment. The range of affections and desires, the intellectual exhilaration of formal arrangement in the verse structures, the lusty grapplings and delicate trembling holdings-still, the decisive grips and tentative handlings, are brilliantly captured again and again, fully alive to the deepest innate contradiction in love. That contradiction is this: you want your beloved to be yours alone, to be forever as she or he is, eternally, but at the same time, you want he or she to be with you in all circumstances, among others, engaging, surprising, taking part in different contexts and arguing, independently-minded, his or her own singular self, and at the same time, joyfully and freely united with you, as one. Your lover is the dancer, and also, the dance itself. Maybe that contradiction is at the heart of the understanding that love is always tenderness and violence, invasion and claiming – a claiming not of property, but of loyalty and respect – and such things are not only claimed but demanded and commanded. And when such acts are matched and reciprocal, the relations implied in the poems, inferred by their readers, may be acknowledged as good.

The most extended series of love poems is the 'Amoretti'. These are evidently once again lyrical and autobiographical but their openness of reference and rigorous formal structures – the sonnet form has its own history and these are highly self-conscious works of poetic artifice – refute the sentimentalism of any claim to singular, unique experience. Who has not been in love? We have all felt like this: 'anxious to be alone' and yet together and separate, and even when in sleep, compelled by the desire 'to keep alive the air we breathe'. Romantic gestures are not foreign here: 'when you kiss / know, as you touch me / the lips of time touch an eternity'. This would be the sort of phrase it would be impossible to use in the degraded common currency of 21st century speech, were it not for the realism that surrounds and imbues it: 'we are old...it is natural to seek the warmth...this day and every day.'

Yet there is ample room for making fun of oneself, the preposterous absurdities of taking things too seriously. A wish to make the 'twitterings of a poem or two' prompts the poet's self-awareness of being, after 'a night of study full of yawns' being 'as dumb as a sick budgie'. And yet also there is the simple sexy sensuality of the shape of a curve: just as a row of eider duck turns on the river Thames,

> I squeeze
> the swell that marks your hip
> under the warm fabric of your coat.

Domestic circumstances, the bedroom, kitchen, living room, the gentle cultivation of the garden over time, fishing and crofting and the return to kitchen, dining room, bedroom – all these are balanced and blend in the condition of love. Self-sufficient aptitude is complemented by the most vulnerable state of dependency, and the self-knowledge of mortal limits, in character and time.

> This sturdy garden on a windswept hill
> would never pass for Eden in this world:
> but when I stand in it and think of you
> who made this happen, then the world is seen
> in this small Eden, gathering all things green.

The wild rose in the north wind gives us hope.

Not only the 'Amoretti' but also the 'Stornelli' carry this on, a practising fondness. And further: there are the 'Cherry-Tree Poems' and poems expressing love of different kinds, for persons in different roles: valentines, birthday poems, family poems, the specifically-designated 'Love Poems' and the semi-surreal, solid but whimsical, imagistically unpredicted 'stone boats' poems.

John Purser completed a PhD on the literary work, the novels and plays, of the greatest of modern Irish artists, Jack Butler Yeats (1871-1957). The dedication of Yeats's kaleidoscope-novel of anecdotes and apercus, *Sligo* (1930), might stand for an essential element in John Purser's work. It is: 'To Venus. I leave it to you mam.'

5.

Love helps or directs, and can misdirect or wreck, your journey through whatever landscape you're given or choose, which brings us to the fifth main theme: geography, terrain or landscape. These words mean different things but the meanings overlap, and suggest different ways of seeing, and of being in and part of, what they mean. In an interview from the early 1990s, the American poet Edward Dorn was asked whether he would consider himself a 'landscape poet'. He replied: 'Nobody could be a landscape poet in the same way that painters are landscape painters. So I'm not, and I don't know anybody who is.' He elaborates on this:

> Landscape is not a poetic device. It is a material thing. You can say, 'Over hill and dale...' Or, 'The rain came down in sheets. Every once in a while it cleared and one could see the black soot of a lonely locomotive traveling toward Aberystwyth.' That's still not landscape. That's just a bunch of words going on about what's out there. If you are on earth, you are on a landscape, and there's nothing much you can do about that.

When pressed further about the idea of 'landscape as a character', he replies:

> You're talking more about 'haunt' actually. That gets to involve the 'human in place.' That's what Lawrence was talking about in 'Reflections on the Death of a Porcupine.' Consequently, that's what Olson was largely talking about. Those things are simple enough. But that's not landscape.

Pressed again further on the significance, if not of landscape, then of 'the local', 'its particular activity and complication today', Dorn says more:

> Both Lawrence and Pound took their intellectual cues from Thomas Hardy, who was the literary giant of their youth. If you follow Lawrence, to have a true local, you have to have gods of the local. You can't have monotheism. It does not tolerate the local. Monotheism is centrality of power and total control.

For Dorn, the idea of monotheism is essentially to do with a lust for 'control and dominance and bullying'. In religious terms, it would be 'a bullying theology. Definitely. I mean its whole strength is intolerance.' But in contrast to this, the 'gods of the local' allow you to exercise respect for, and participation in, what your immediate context is.

This principle of sensitivity to the local and responsibility for its priorities as well as your own, inhabits John Purser's poems. They are not painterly depictions but aspects of engagement. Let me push this further.

In an essay entitled 'A Story for Aesop', John Berger talks about 'the *address* of the landscape', signifiying the meaning of place as it is experienced not only in its daily visualisation but also in its economic, physical and social relations with the people who live in it, upon it, and through it, across generations. This is how the landscape addresses you. And it is different, in different places. The 'address' of a South American tropical forest is very different from that of a North African desert; cities, towns and villages generate their own forms of address; and in the land- and seascapes of the west coast of Scotland, and Ireland, particularly, it makes accurate sense to talk of what Dorn calls a 'haunt' because the idea of a haunted place has an actual reality in the fact of tides receding and returning, in perpetual rhythm over days, months, seasons, decades, millennia.

This understanding of geography and inhabited terrain is characteristic of Purser's poetry, wherever he is, be it Skye or the east coast of North America. This is not merely a poetry of tourism or of 'postcards home'. It is rather the sense that wherever people live, there is this capacity of life to be understood, to be sensitive towards. Charles Olson once wrote that SPACE (writ big) is characteristic of 'man born in America' and perhaps the truth in that imbues the national, or even the imperial, self-apprehension of the United States. There are similar ways to generalise about different national identities and some of Purser's poems do this, but mainly they are much more to do with locality. He writes of particular places on the Isle of Skye, rather than of the comprehensive, multiple, various, singular nationality we call Scotland. His poems are therefore much more works of fidelity to locality rather than engagements with the theory of politics or the posturing of political assertions.

The 'New World Poems' are exhilarating and tentative evocations of the experience of discovery, where familiar literary reference ('what once was Prospero's island') and human knowledge ('our own youth catching us by heart and hand') go along with respectful annotation of different geographies, placenames, languages, ways of meaning: 'Nashawana' brings 'the muffled sound / of a bell-buoy lurching distantly / in fog'). In such fog of unfamiliar territory, the poet is 'surrounded by birds I cannot name' and reflects, 'How ignorant I must seem to them.' Nevertheless, birds, friends, shorelines, ships, the working human economy, deliver things that make communication, comprehension, possible:

> At Tarpaulin Cove a fine two-master
> rides at anchor, floating on the fog.

The vanity of Merrill's Monument, 'the browned bodies of practiced women / sailing by in splendid yachts' are signals of a human fact we will find in every country.

6.

And yet, the orientation is to turn us towards the North, and the residence is settled, again and again, in 'Northern Latitudes'. This is one of the key poems in the book, beginning with the reference to 'They' – people who have 'made their compromise / with all their origins / on tougher rock'. Compromise and negotiation may be our human need and fact, but hard rock is our stony foundation, and the poem tells us that 'They' – these people in whose company Purser locates himself – are well aware of what tragedy means, the possibility that 'germination die / within the seed.' In its brief statements the poem summarises so much of Scottish, or even more broadly, north European, winter people:

> they tighten their religion,
> clean the wells,
> and dig fertility
> into the ground,
> knowing the ice may yet return

This gives a sense of locality not only in place but also through deepening roots in time, through historical millennia. Fiona Stafford, in her book *Local Attachments: The Province of Poetry* (2010), says this:

'The vital significance of local attachments for art arises from truth's need for strong foundations.' Talking of Robert Burns, especially with reference to the Kilmarnock edition of his poems, she elaborates: 'It was as if the poet found himself through his perception of others, while his sense of the ground he occupied was almost always shared ground.'

In the 20th century, Hugh MacDiarmid heralded his commitment to 'local attachment' – but in terms of his political commitment to national political independence for Scotland, he was not a 'local' poet, even though the Borders, and later, Shetland, were geographical localities which deeply informed his writing. It was that generation of poets who were working after the Second World War, who could be described more correctly as poets of 'local attachment' – George Mackay Brown, Iain Crichton Smith, Sorley MacLean, Norman MacCaig, Robert Garioch, Edwin Morgan and others – and in the generation that has followed them, the most conspicuous reconfiguration has been in terms of gendered identity, the poetic articulation of the experiences, perspectives and understanding of women, especially in the work of Liz Lochhead, Kathleen Jamie, Jackie Kay, Meg Bateman and Janet Paisley. Still, the general significance of Fiona Stafford's perception applies to all three generations, and 'local attachments' can be read into the work of each of them. John Purser's poems span the second and third of these three generations, and helpfully complicate the scene. The truth in Stafford's formulation resides in its endorsement of a more general observation about cultural identity, its need for specific reference. This is as true of Douglas Dunn as of Ian Hamilton Finlay, of Edwin Muir as of Carol Ann Duffy. And in this more comprehensive understanding, Purser's work comprises a significant and singular character.

No-one but he could have written the group of poems entitled 'Six Composers'. He is of course a great musicologist. Or put it this way: John Purser is the most important historian of Scottish music there has ever been. His magnum opus, *Scotland's Music: A History of the Traditional and Classical Music of Scotland from Early Times to the Present Day* (Edinburgh: Mainstream, 1992; revised edition, 2007), is a book that should be widely available and borrowed regularly from every library and used in every school, college and university in Scotland. Despite the accolades it was awarded, it remains neglected in the current cultural climate, and is out of print in 2014. It arose from the series of programmes Purser wrote and presented for BBC Radio Scotland, and since their first broadcast in 1992 in a series of thirty programmes, each one, one-and-a-half hours long, then in a new version in 2007 of fifty half-hour programmes, an increasing number of professional CD recordings have been made available of performances of Scottish music by world-class orchestras and choirs with conductors of international reputation. Yet so much of Scotland's serious music has not been accepted into the classical concert repertoire, and as a national archive which might be listened to by a nation's people, and internationally, Scotland's most serious, classical, music remains almost unknown.

'Six Composers' is a group of poems that stay vivid and sharp, deeply perceptive portraits of six of the major composers in the history of Scotland's music, each one a character who would have been worth knowing. The poems evoke them in their own time and among their own musical and personal ethos: William Kinloch (flourished around 1600), composer and spy, living in a world of secrets, with Mary Queen of Scots and Queen Elizabeth of England at either end of the spectrum. Kinloch had to negotiate carefully through writing pavanes, galliards, and the piece entitled 'The Hunt's Up'. He enters Purser's poem at its beginning in a sinister, cautious way:

> Sshh! It's not safe here. The curtain swells;
> a door has opened down the corridor;
> whispers of music follow whoever walks
> along these carpets of secrets...
> and there you sit,
> your fingers are articulating thoughts
> that none dare say aloud.

John Blackwood McEwen (1868-1948), brilliant writer of string quartets and orchestral tone poems embodying the ballads and the Galloway of his youth, living through the tragedies of two world wars, writing piano music to match the Scottish Colourists' work in painting in France, then returning to regenerate a musical vision of Scotland, and, in the String Quartet 'Threnody', setting the traditional lament, 'The Flowers of the Forest' in a way no composer from any other nation ever could, an elegy and wordless song of grief for the wasted lives of World War One. This work is as important as, in literature, Lewis Grassic Gibbon's *Sunset Song* – we all should know it deeply.

Alexander Campbell Mackenzie (1847-1935) should be as familiar to Scots as Elgar is to the English. They were friends, and knew each other's greatness. A master of the orchestra, in violin and piano concertos, orchestral works such as the heartbreakingly beautiful 'Benedictus' and the still almost-unknown oratorios, Mackenzie's achievement is formidable, warm as Brahms can be, poignant and lonely at times as Elgar himself, but full of heart and substance. Purser evokes his companionable presence in a way that is true to the music.

Erik Chisholm (1904-65), Scottish modernist, scholar and friend of Bartók, massively productive and experimental, 'Giving more to others than you ever gave yourself'. The poem should be read along with Purser's biography of the man, *Erik Chisholm: Chasing a Restless Muse* (2009).

The most generous of spirits, he died far too young. As did Michael Marra (1952-2012). Purser's portrait of him delivers his character and spirit, his animal mischief, his sense of dance and song.

The biography of Hamish MacCunn (1868-1916) is in his portrait, and the spirit of his character – he once matched verbal wit with George Bernard Shaw, crossed swords in print, and MacCunn was the winner, hands down. He also died too young, of cancer of the throat, but in the last lines Purser gives him, still lives on, defiant and victorious:

> I am here, coughing
> beneath the shadow of Cìr Mhòr –
> and Slàinte Mhath! Good health! My glass is full.
> The one thing left to do is empty it.

As Purser writes in 'It Is Dusk', even while the blackbird sings

> in virtuosic clarity
> as the light dims we are all subsumed
> into the gentle silence of the night.

The portraits are not elegies, though, and – prophetic thought – it is not night that claims them – but rather they are dialogues and voices, personae of composers whose time is yet to come.

> This is Scotland.
> I am Scots.

And despite their isolation from so many music lovers now, many of us have been introduced to their music through John Purser's work as musicologist, and Mackenzie, MacCunn and McEwen knew each other personally. Theirs – and ours – is a community of purpose, and a sense of shared intent, and critical interest, and surely, love. We are in good company, with them. This is, and stays, important.

All of these poems are exercises in orientation, exploring northern latitudes and finding ways to inhabit them more fully. This is also true of Purser's musical compositions, collected in three CDs, *Bannockburn* (JWP030), *Circus Suite* (JWP020) and *Dreaming of Islands* (JWP010). The range of compositions to be found here complements the poems in this book and the scholarly work of retrieval and renewal his archaeology of Scotland's music has brought up from history. Moreover, the recurring themes of the poems can be heard in the music as well, the dialogues and addresses are present in such compositions as 'The Old Composer Remembers' and 'A Message to Hirini Melbourne' and 'In Memoriam Hirini Melbourne'; the terrain upon which our selfhood is determined is there in 'Bannockburn'; the intimate physicality of inside and outside in 'Throat'; the singular blend and balance of humour and deadly seriousness in 'Carrier Strike'; the geographical evocations are in 'Skyelines' and 'Dreaming of Islands' and the profundity of love is to be heard in 'Creagan Beaga' (to complement a poem by Sorley MacLean) and 'Tha thu air aigeann m'intinn' (You are at the bottom of my mind', complementing a poem by Iain Crichton Smith), and above all perhaps, in 'Luis' (the rowan tree, in Gaelic, the tree that gives protection).

7.

The monologues of, or addresses to, the six composers, prompt further thought on Fiona Stafford's observation that Burns found himself through his perception of others, of recognising and negotiating shared ground. For Purser, this is most evident in the dialogues he has with the dedicatees of his 'Dedicatatory Poems': among them the great Gaelic poet Sorley MacLean, the composer and pioneering radio producer Martin Dalby, the artist Jack Yeats, and the couple Kay and El Forbes, about to retire to a new home on the banks of the Charles River, and to whom he gives wise advice:

> At the closing of the door leave no regrets:
> slacken the guy-ropes, tug out the rooted pegs,
> strap up the costume cases, buckle to
> the basketful of properties, cease pacing those fine floor-boards...

Their sculpted horse with foreleg raised will go 'to pace / new ramparts in defence of our first freedoms' while the couple, from now on, may

> look abroad with equanimity
> on the unreasoning river, knowing that where it goes
> is where city to nature, body to spirit flows.

Body moving to spirit is there in the bird poems. These are masterpieces of close observation and sympathetic emulations in words of the spirits that move the physical creatures themselves.

In 'Champion' the poet is out on a boat with his gun, hunting skart. He tells us that his 'eye is in' – he's on form, balanced, accurate, and shoots to kill, meat for the pot. This is not sport but hunting for food. But this time, in a fantastic and utterly convincing parable, the bird evades him, shot after shot, diving and resurfacing, knowing that what's balanced is its own increasing exhaustion after such effort, and the gunman's growing sense of admiration for its smeddum, its determination to defy and survive. In the end, the bird is nature, knows its victory requires no show of triumph. He is faster than anything a man can do. The first line of 'Snow Bunting' sums it up, perhaps: 'beyond all hope of life you are alive' – the human interloper can only hope that his words

> will, like the snow bunting, find a home
> in desolate places where no one
> should be alone.

And the skylark prompts the question:

> who can unstitch a stretch of sky
> and with the same song seam it up again,
> or tirl the air and needle into notes
> a trillion tiny ear-drum taps
> with threaded light

Seen in the world of the crofter at work, the poem, like Burns in 'To a Mouse', looking forward, but unlike Burns, not fearfully, concludes: 'when you fly free and I'm left cutting peat / against a winter half a year away...'

> I raise my hat and yield the gods a grin
> as proof that all creation's crazy made.

All creation sets in more grimly in the 'Poems and Dialogues Concerning Natural Religion'. We come now to the essence of the matter. This is the ultimate other, the poet is brought into dialogue with God, most centrally in 'Ranging':

> See how the bells are set, their heads up,
> tongues in cheeks – a silent innocence
> poised between prime and evensong.

Climbing up to them, a closer view reveals them:

> Massive: immutable. Man, woman, child; each
> an allowance to release their souls:
> Look down. You see each sally hangs
> from a wheel of fortune: we play games
> with magic numbers – caters,
> bob and peal, royal and maximus.
> You say they shout of laughter;
> joy and love? When I'm alone
> I clamber through these bells
> and hear them cry to God – silent,
> vibrant, intense. I tell you
> they have primed eternity
> to hunt us down.
> They have us in their minds.

This is I think a terrific poem, one of the best in the book, one for the anthologies. God and predestination and form, music that might dominate and lead all to destruction, or liberate and open up all possible good things, the sheer and simple confrontation here, free will and nature, joy and sorrow, the lives and what are natural, or else unnatural, deaths – all these return us to Edward Dorn's distinction between monotheism and gods of the local. Purser's respect for the pluralities of identity subverts or precludes the tyrannical authority of any single purpose or authoritarian power – whether that is defined in the state, the church, empire, Royalty or Divinity. For Purser, power arises from matter through spirit, and cannot be held or owned as property. It must be acknowledged and worked with, in nature. And this makes his dedicated poems not only tributes but purposeful invocations of acknowledgement. And it fuels these dialogue poems with a depth and urgency some of the more whimsical, pleasurable and occasional poems elsewhere in the book do not require. Where seriousness is needed, it is supplied. You don't take poems like these lightly.

This section begins satirically, comically, though, as Jehovah's witnesses are confronted with an unexpectedly argumentative interlocutor who overturns their assertions firmly, playfully and methodically, with admirable patience and care, regretting only that he could not tempt them either with apples or biscuits, knowing that even biscuits would have been enough. They walk away with their reductive and closed minds and attitudes, are sent firmly back, over the horizon. But the seriousness that underlies this confrontation imbues the Columba poems, 'Columba to God', 'Columba to King David' and 'Columba and Saint Finnan'. In each, song is the key, and birdsong ends the third – consoling, or mocking? The ambiguity is scary. The human words end with a question: 'what have you to say?' The birdsong answers it, or leaves it unanswered: who can say? But the sympathetic spirit of Columba in the first two poems in this triptych is firm, heartfelt, real. Even so, the doubt remains:

> I too have cast my voice
> beyond our mortalities.
> Has anybody heard?

'Ranging' leads on to the dialogues with David Hume, the refutations of Bishop Berkeley and Plato, the return to earth in its October hills and the hot coal of truth, but the governing principle here is in 'Ballade for the Duke of Orleans': 'we men, and women, were not born for pain'. The tragic loves of the Celtic figures, Deirdre, and Gráinne and Diarmait, are there, no question, but the Pelagian heresy is affirmed, cheerfully, in 'Botticelli to Venus':

> I see you step
> naked ashore; frank, touching, unashamed,
> fresh from the scallop in the willow skep

> through whose old uprights of despair and rage
> I've woven hope, so men might catch and sow
> the seeds of oceans – but where people grow.

At the centre of this section of the book there is 'The Translator Confesses to the Book of Books' and in this poem, perhaps, the manifesto of creative transformation, the open secret fact that binds together art and nature, is given. The poet, the translator, the artist of whatever kind, begins: 'I pick my words. I keep them scrupulous, clean / and comprehensible.' But there is a 'sharp key / that feels for intimacy, truth, The Word' and the tumblers have fallen further as the small and feeble things that make us human will corrupt us. But defeat itself is what rattles the padlock at the gate, calling for

> someone to come and help devise
> the words to fit the wards of paradise.

The compromised world is where we are, as Sorley MacLean said of W.B. Yeats: 'You had the chance, William, the chance for your words...' Even while the ideal was there, 'you had your excuse / for every man has his excuse' – or to put it in Wordsworth's phrase, there is this 'still sad music of humanity' – which is why we need the rowan tree.

John Purser's poems have much in common with the two greatest Gaelic poems of the 18th century, Duncan Ban MacIntyre's 'Praise of Ben Dorain' and Alastair MacMhaighstir Alasdair's 'The Birlinn of Clanranald'. These poems are far away from us in sensibility and time, but they are important.

What they share with the ethos of the poems of John Purser, I can describe like this:

'Praise of Ben Dorain' creates an ethos of human beings in the natural world, in relation to nature, dominating nature in some respects, at its mercy in others. There are what might be called 'gods of the local' – specific absolute authorities pertaining to time, place, living beings and their relations – and there is the imposing dominant authority of mortality. Therefore, at the forefront of our experience are what we might call ecological relations, the relations between matters of violence and care, or indeed love, and the equilibrium between things that is reinforced through experiences of violence and caring, tenderness, responsibility. We are made forcefully aware of the boundaries and borders that distinguish things, and the acts of violence or community that break those boundaries and cross those borders. Such acts bring about permanent alteration in some respects (literally, living things may be cared for, knowingly, or they may be killed, mercifully); but also, such acts may be seasonal or cyclical.

Yet what Purser's poems are knowing about is something 'Praise of Ben Dorain' does not deal with, the possibility of permanent alteration on a far greater scale. Duncan Ban MacIntyre could not foresee in his poem the loss of all the deer, or the entire clearance of people from his favoured location, but these things happened, and at a later date, he returned to see the waste that had been made of his heavenly mountain. Purser lives and writes two centuries later, and the waste and devastations of the 20th century are recent history for him. And yet his poems connect with the deeper sustaining priorities that remain, that are still present in 'Praise of Ben Dorain' and as clearly seen in John Purser's vision as well.

Arguably, this brings him even closer to 'The Birlinn of Clanranald'. This poem describes the working ship, the birlinn, its component parts, sails, tiller, oars, and so on, its sixteen crewmen, each with their appointed role and place, and it describes their mutual working together, rowing, and then sailing out to sea, from South Uist over to Carrickfergus in Ireland. The last third of the poem is an astonishing, terrifying, exhilarating description of the men and the ship in a terrible storm that blows up, threatens to destroy them, and which they pass through, only just making it to safe harbour, mooring and shelter. The poem is so visceral and grainy in its depiction of realities, it almost seems hostile to metaphoric interpretation, just as Purser's poems seem to prioritise the actual over the imaginary, or metaphorical. But there is another interpretation of 'The Birlinn of Clanranald' which its historical context suggests, without straining the purpose of metaphoric implication too far.

Both poems, 'Ben Dorain' and 'The Birlinn', were composed in the aftermath of the Jacobite rising of 1745 and the massacre at Culloden in 1746, and their authors were engaged on opposite sides of that conflict, though Duncan Ban, in service to the Hanoverian Campbells, could not accept the rightness of the fight, and famously discarded his laird's sword. It is possible that both poems reflect upon this social and human disaster in ways that go further than their literal meanings.

'Praise of Ben Dorain' is a panegyric, a traditional praise-song, but what is praised is not a clan chief but an ecology of value. The clan structure is absent from the poem, and in this respect it is quite singular in the Gaelic poetry of its time. 'The Birlinn of Clanranald' presents a clan and a crew of men working in extreme co-ordination, disciplined and intuitive, in conditions of knowledge drawn from experience, but they and their vessel are subjected to a storm of unprecedented violence, a natural imposition that calls up inimical forces from well beyond anything that might have been predicted. The courage and skills of the crew and the strength of the ship carry them through, but at a cost, and without any sense of inevitability. The safe harbour they come to is in Ireland, and the connection between the Celtic west of Scotland and the Irish coast their voyage makes, is, also, a signal of an ancient kinship, across differences, of the Celtic peoples and the human needs of all people, as opposed to inimical forces in nature and anti-human forces in the political world that intervene to wreak havoc and destruction on us all.

These inimical forces are always there, ready to break into the worlds we might make for ourselves, family, friends, companions. Human greed and vanity deregulate or restructure the world and our best responses to it. This is as true today as ever. But in poems and music, paintings and sculptures, the structures of ships and the architecture, and work, of crofts and dwelling-places, art of all kinds, there are ways to oppose and resist those natural and unnatural impositions. The appetite for self-extension is humanly healthy, but never to the point of vanity or bloated self-regard.

In this respect, John Purser's work is based upon the premise of the accepted limits of necessity, and the noble work of pushing against them all. It is therefore profoundly anti-Romantic, and absolutely not transgressive. In his work, as with some of the great Gaelic poems in a long tradition, the aesthetics of nature *are* the politics of nature, a 'poetics' of the environment. Through the living creatures in the poems and the movements of the poems themselves, his work moves not 'towards' but 'within' a poetics of the environment.

And yet it could have been written by nobody else.

The sensibility from which these poems arise is therefore to be understood as belonging to that of a larger company of writers, artists and thinkers, people of all kinds, quite different from the conventions of celebrity culture, the commercialisation of commodities, even commodities almost without value in monetary, material terms. 'Not many people read poetry,' William Carlos Williams once noted, 'but a lot of people are dying for the want of what they might find in it.'

So despite the hard-headed understanding of reality that imbues this book with a character of measurement and a generous disposition, there is also a capacity for romantic gesture, not to be denied, at the right times, in the right moments. And this is nowhere more evident than in the poem that gives the title to the book, 'Homage to Jack Yeats'. We have noted him before, and Purser's critical appraisal of his literary works. In this poem, the subject is one of his greatest paintings: 'There Is No Night' (1949). Images of it can be found online and the picture is easily seen, in our age of mechanical reproduction, but the experience of standing before the actual painting is not the same as that of sitting in front of a computer screen, so it is worth making the pilgrimage to the Dublin City Gallery, the Hugh Lane, in Ireland, to do that.

The title seems to refer to the Bible, the book of Revelation, 22.5: 'There will be no more night. They will not need the light of a lamp or the light of the sun, for the Lord God will give them light. And they will reign for ever and ever.' But the painting does not need the Bible reference, for it arises from a pre-Christian sense of humanity that connects to the Celtic world, far older than Christ. This is the world of the horse, the world of Ossian, Finn MacCoul and the Fianna. Travelling through 'ignorant lands', 'the white horse' running, and 'the shadow man', rising from rest, may find or carry a 'strange salvation' for us, to us. Dawn – revelation – is always rolling round, somewhere on the point of reappearing, and:

> they have seen before the dawn and,
> in the long day-span
> of the north summer light,
> know, now and forever,
> there is no night.

The painting, and the poem made from it, are a summons, a way of reaching beyond the self, to receive and give, 'due homage'. And to 'see other and beyond,'

All John Purser's poems, all his compositions and scholarship, indeed, are part of this, made to be given, for us to receive, to learn from, to sleep 'no more / than needful', and now, to rise.

In the Manuscript Room of the Library

Everything's a tree:
the curl of paper
the parquet floor
the desk-grain and the doorway
the catalogue cabinet's wood
the hat-rack and the roof.
The sounds are trees:
chairs creek
leaves rustle
someone sighs
now and then one whispers
as the keeper, sheltering, bows
over a query.

Readers search like grubs
under the bark of books
shedding skin and hair:
a little draught
lifts wisps
from an old lady's chevelure
strayed from its loosening knot:
fingers rub foreheads
there is a scratch of pens
of branch and twig
scrabbling to set free
the deep concentric memory
in the tree.

The Laughter of the Sea (from *Six Sea Poems* by Sean Purser)

I

Furred with frost, beside the path,
Little poles of grass conduct
The foot along. Here leaves lie flattened
Clammy brown, with whitened veins,
Here a stream, unfrozen still,
Crosses the path, and tumbles straight
Into the bushes.

After that you round a bend
And the sudden sea displayed
Ripples in the sudden sunlight,
Miles on glittering miles of light,
Scattered back to the sky;
Looking like laughter to the eye,
Raising feelings like laughter in the heart.

The sea whose currents lick
Round continents, and flow
Underneath the ice-capped pole,
Raise storms of wind
In sleepy coves, and hurl blue tons
Of water on the rocks,
Now in the winter sun
Coils sparkling, and makes laughter seem
The rule and truth of things,
Makes sunlight and laughter seem the truth
And rule of things for ever.

Crofting Poems

Wooden Tongue

When the wind changed
she moved down towards the woods
for shelter. No doubt the sheds were full.
Her last late calf
had sucked at her too long
and, rather than extend
her famine, she was shot.
The round hole in her head
was pink and white
against the coarse black of her hair.
And with the larks everywhere
and long spring sunlight
in the trees, our spades
dug up the bluebell bulbs
to hide her bloated frame.
There was much washing of hands
but no one would take tea,
finding more comfort in the steps
of that morning's new brown calf.
And, in our separation, we were all
left inarticulate as beasts.

A Share of the Wind

We sag about the shed
and, panting, watch this black
stretched calf, the rope
we used to draw him out
still knotted round his hooves.
The torch flicks uselessly
at his dead tongue. He's spent.
The dab of forefinger
can scarcely shift his eyeball.

So in the dark draughts
of the drystone walls
I put my mouth to his wet mouth
and hear his lungs puff – oh
so easily – blow gently –
till he breathes alone,
rattling, though sure.

But, straw-rubbed, with my smell,
she does not know her first possession
as her own. We salt his hide:
and soon she licks him down, her tongue
in earnest tearing and nudging him,
massaging limbs and heart
and shivering flank.
Look now how good she is to him.

Born into a week of gales,
all these surviving instincts
draw me in: am I not
life to life now joined to him
by rope and salt and air and touch of tongues:
have we not now a share of the wind?

When the bolt bangs at his brain
will I, too, gasp –
and will my head feel pain?

White Rainbow

This is a magic mist
no doubt of it

on its full tide
a satiate sea

still yields fat fish
gullet and gut filled

to sparkling lures
fantastic feathers

there is sun yet to make
a true white rainbow

charmed arc of light
companioning the boat.

There is a madness in it all
the boat's slow dance

the fish scales glittering
on our coats, the white arc

magical, the charmed
life, breathing deep.

*Note: A fine mist will create a white rainbow by diffraction, causing
an overlap of all the colour bands. It is a rare phenomenon, but is not
uncommonly seen from aircraft.*

Sore Udder in Summer

Poor cow,
so now
you fear
to hear
my call,
let fall
your milk,
white silk
in pail,
your tail
on brim
to skim
the steam.
I cream
your teat;
you eat
the flies,
your eyes
half shut,
your cut
a swarm:
no form
of rest.
At best
we nip
and whip
the clegs
from legs
and flank,
each tank
of cud
our blood.
We live
by give
and take
and ache
with hurt
of curt

back-kick
and stick
on hip.
I grip
my hate –
our state
of mind
half blind,
half mad.
We've had
enough.

Cleaning the Net

The tangled net
draped on a bamboo pole
fizzes with struggling crabs
still clinging on
after a tide's time
drawn up from the sea.

There is only one way to free them.
Little as they are
they must be crushed alive
and it is troublesome to smash them with a stick.
I clasp one between thumb
and forefinger
his free claw
clawing at my skin:
with a firm pincer movement
I must squeeze the carapace
till it splinters, squirting
fluid in my face.

Next, seaweed
as tenacious in its way.

The net, its pattern now restored,
is stripped clean
bar tentacles of jellyfish
skin stinging but
too fine to be seen.

Truly this task
is utterly opposed
to the immaculate –
but is there not
in the more knowing ways
of those who gather
and must deal with death
something that might be called
brute sensitive,

nursemaids to appetite
knowing we're all caught
in this spotted pattern
and one day
will be hauled in,
some suffocated
and some crushed to death,
and a few desperadoes
tangled widdershins?

Archie

From the blue boat with double prow
we lift the spilling fish-box to the rocks
to clean and fillet; as my knife edge grinds
against the spine, the head lifts
and the mouth forms to an 'O'
silent, before the air sac
breaches with a sigh.

Archie, who can't well speak
the daft thoughts in his mind,
watches, shifting weight
from leg to leg, like an old gull,
though now they scream about us
for their share of heads and guts
and rich fawn-coloured livers – I recall
a man at Mallaig guiding fish
in a receiving tank from the great tear-drop nets;
fighting the gulls with his affectionate roar
and sweep of arm, useless
to stop them perching on his head
or burying the fish beyond his grasp
under a plethora of wings.

Archie, given a chance,
will take all that he can –
from a good sharing of the catch
to cuddles with some scared embarrassed wife.
Frustrated, his abuse echoes off outcrops
of the rock, is heard in every home.

But they tolerate his protest – he is more
than tolerated – understood to be
as necessary as the gulls themselves,
for who knows but one day
his strange, half-innocent brain
will lead them, like the seabirds,
to a place where the heart's fish
are gathered to the shore so plentiful

that the wild combat, laughter and white wings
will fill his isolation with their love
and silence all the protest of his mind.

Mastitis

This is the second calf
that she has lost –
one teat is blind already
and, were that not enough,
her udder now is swollen
hard, lopsided like a gourd.
Her eyes inquire.
It takes more than pity
to stomach milking her.
One must accept
waste spilt on waste
as what she has to give
slashes the grass with red.
Her ears lie low. She kicks.
They say that anyway
it's sure to burst,
and as I press my head
into her side, use her
for shelter and abuse
her bulging teats,
I must accept
that I have learnt to keep
my own acknowledgement
of pain and misery
suppressed, have learnt
to teach my hands
brute ignorance.

Aristocracy

Two princeling sea-trout
hanging by their gills
from first and second finger
have caved in without resistance.

The net, the capture,
humiliation, no returning home
gloriously to spawn,
no explanation ever acceptable,
nothing to do but die;

while a coarse wrangler of a wrass
struggles and jerks free.

I grab him in my fist
squeezing his gut protest

and on the cold marble table, where
he does not jerk or spasm
but battles still for oxygen,

karate chop him near the brain
and gut him while
he's still too dazed to gasp.

The Incorruptible Crofter

He wore a ring upon his hand,
gold, hall-marked as a chastity-band:
he did not lose it in the bed,
but at the peats lost it instead –

it slipped his finger, be it told –
this silly circle of dull gold,
not incorruptible, but soft,
had worn, as it's not fit to croft.

Now there's a moral in these lines: –
the ring confuses and combines
adventure with cupidity
and honest labour with stupidity:
for gold, the emblem of the rich,
has little virtue in a ditch.

Arthritis

Where she lies now,
the damp pressed to her hide,
the ground has taken on the shape
of her left side and has
already closed that eye.

We dig a pit beside her in the peat,
impatient for the gun, and think
if only she could walk
until the autumn cattle sales
there might be profit in her yet,
though, having used her up,
who calls us to account?

November from the Clach Rathad

The Canna lighthouse, smearing out the sky
of soft grey half way indigo,
talks to Tex Geddes on the coast of Rum,
his masthead light now making steady north
for Soay harbour on a full flood tide:
a car – just headlamps on a hill –
plunges from skyline down to Tarskavaig,
and a daft dog in Drinan barks
at the sudden shadow of a black cow's bulk;
a blackbird stutters and a snipe
startles along the shadowed ditch.
It is the time when searches are abandoned,
when the doe rabbit I stunned against a stone
shivers suddenly long past her death;
and the tilted landscape,
like a capsized sail, dips into the sea
of northern latitude so deep in indigo
it seems we'll never right ourselves
before Orion swings into the dark
certain to hunt us down.

Near Eniskillen

I am on the banks of Lower Lough Erne.
Evening is on its way.
The cars and motorboats have gone to bed
and mankind has gone to its televisions.

All would be silent, save for the slap
of little waves on the thin shingle,
were it not
that cattle are calling across the lough.
Some are lonely. Some are in need of sex.
Some are related and are calling across not just water
but many fence lines and a good few roads
down which they were driven
one way or the other
separating them from their own families.

Across from where I sit increasingly chilled
on the little jetty, is White Island.
It is home to stone bishops and a Sheila-na-gig
whose private parts are most publicly displayed.
She holds her pudenda as wide open as is possible.
She needs a man.

White Island is a bull island;
where you put bulls to manage their mating.
These things have to be done properly.

And still the little waves slap and splash
on the thin shingle,
and the cattle keep calling
right into the dark,
until I too retreat
into the constraining habitat
of man.

Grass Snake

I've seen him often on the path,
dark, subtle-flecked,
his scales oily and laminate
as the black shale
among his native rocks.
I keep him secret. If I told,
people would scorch him out,
strike him with sticks.

Today, returning up the hill,
I see him motionless,
but changed.

I must have stood on him unknowing –
all his slim beauty marred
by that one kink
in his flexive back
now paralysed in pain.

Noiseless, he looks at me,
not knowing, not knowing
will I strike again.

Glen Scaladal

I trudge the ridge and furrow
of old lazy-beds: the loss and gain
where the cas-crom, heavy hilted,
long-footed, drained the land.
Now the land weeps, deserted,
choked with rain.

These written griefs
frowning and weeping
through the green-glowing glen
remain unspoken:
they are home for the iris,
stately and fine,
and burial ditch for the spent ewe,
her loins plundered by foxes –
the torn womb reveals
a small wet eyeless head.

There are no children here
whose supple hands
would have been asked to ease
that hard delivery:
and thinking of the lambs, I hear
the voice of a child running, mad-cap
to her mother's woolen skirt
across sunlit Glen Scaladal,
and in that cry the perilous call
that searches still
for the warm comfort of humanity.

Croftwork

The twin died overnight
despite all efforts, feeding colostrum
at the cost of near impalement
on his mother's horns,
her patience none the less astonishing.
The other's in the shed, hand cossetted.

Next morning, when I hear his throaty cry,
a cow runs frantic
towards where his mother stands indifferent,
or wise to the reality.

I open the half door and step in.
He's left his hay and carpet bed and sprawls
helpless on the dry cement,
convulsing, froth around his lips.

Unlock the locker.
Draw out the gun: select
a double zero cartridge from the belt.

Another calf cry as his body twists,
legs spasmodic.

Choose the top barrel:
slide the safety catch and place
the muzzle in between his eyes
just touching calf-soft hair.
Select the second trigger.
Squeeze.

The force flings half his body through an arc:
the young pink blood flows smooth
and silent, and coagulates.

Good gun the merciful.

If such a day should come to me,
give me a soldier's kind deliverance.
Come close: aim straight:
and wash away my thoughts before they dry.

The Counting Stick

The Counting Stick

As each sheep passes to the pen
he marks a notch, a ring
for every goat, diamonds for ten.
He cuts them in the bark
of chestnut staves and peels
the old skin from the life
of green-moist sapwood.
Napes jolt at the tug of teeth
on dusty fodder;
the clappers on the neck-bells
tint the air copper as the goats
pass by, anachronistic
as the tilted eye on the sun's
altitude, the angle of the hand.

But when they walled his school
he learned to count
more than his fingers and his flocks.
Notch, ring and diamond spiral
from the point and pattern hours,
hoggets, tups and ewes obliterated
by the new design he seeks
to regulate. His knife is noiseless
as the strips and chips are lost
into the grass, each one
a nick of time.

The sound of copper
chinks within his hand.
He has employment,
like the soldier on the round
of the mechanical clock
above the city square. They're both
awry. Stiff drill should be
abandoned in a war:
against both scythe and sand
the counting stick
was more essential than this ritual
and, though discarded still, still,
still marks time.

In the quarry a man cuts
millenia with no more thought
than a flat chisel growing
from his hand, a hammer
held to drop, instinctively
he uses time, his ear on time
to catch cracks in the ring
and measure his own pulse in pulse
of blows reviving the rock's heart
to sound the murmur in the fault,
renewing death in an autopsy
of the earth.

And as he climbs past centuries
of sediments, exposed
on the cliff face –
the flecks of fossils
still to undergo
another metamorphosis –
the impulse of his lungs
staggers as each step
passes a life to that same life
evolved, exposing his precarious
hold on earth, impermanent,
the surmise of his breath.

So he makes fossils of his kind,
statues in marble, figurines
in clay, fingers indented
on the thigh of her he models,
in extension, marking
paternity as he inserts
the shaft between these limbs
of stone, new-sweating
in the sun. Her welcome
will evaporate, her limbs
become dead progeny and life
and death, thus introduced,

leave her as host to meet
her menopause. Her salt blood
calcifies. She is laid down
by tides, embedded by the moon,
the marble cuckoo-clock.

And yet the uniformity
of hours, pointed and ordering
acceptance without grace,
seems a poor innovation
in chronology.
The old stark vertical,
the counting stick, thrust
in the earth, had more
of subtlety – extending hours
at sunset and sunrise.
A man could work more in the shade,
stretch out the limbs of time,
and recognise morning and evening
as eternities and noon
his consummation that was lived
in the awaiting and remembering.

But he is paced within the arc of hands;
his fortune is pricked out
by a stray needle darting
between poles.
The sun plays rings
around the compass rose, and falling,
falling on the drum of rain,
shadows his latitude, now ruled
along the gnomon's edge; –
the dial fans the hours
and leaves his time of sleep unmarked.

At the hub of paths he seeks,
among the haze-blue of preserving herbs,
cures for old age – borage, mint
and thyme. The sun-clock spins the world

around the beds: and yet
the stasis of each radius
is illusion; in this sink of heat
the garden spirals and the world is still.
This vortex of the hours focusses
the spinning needles in the flesh,
sustains the hum of motion
in the dragon-fly, weaving air:
the eye is shuttled with its weft
and settled in the shed of age appeased
by the unresting molecule of warmth
dancing within its sphere.

Songs of Occupation

The Organist Confesses to His Mirror

God knows, I've looked in you enough;
bride after bride has walked into my eye;
I've held them, hurried them, desired them
too in all unholy ways; but you are wise
to turn a blind eye to your back
for here from pedal-board to flues
I've played out more than fantasies
and fugues. I've spurned disasters
in the choir, old hymns for old souls,
ageing anthems, unannounced
I've made my alterations to their sense,
twisted progressions and, in extremis,
let the bellows roar full organ impious
extravagance of wind and reed – nature,
true nature, is an appetite for living and,
by Christ, I've put that shudder
to their limbs and stirred the church
from gratings between pews
to the fan-vaulting boss. Ah, yes –
but I have held the quiet like a thread,
a note so long that there was time
to trace it through the transepts, down the aisles,
mirrored and echoing, while I
half sit and slide upon my bench,
feet pattering like puppets on the wood,
fingers precise – expression here
is executing notes, each digit lifted,
knowing when to stop. Switch off. Switch out
the lights. On leaving, look behind and check –
my life is scattered here in whisperings,
broken cobwebs – lock the door.

Lines for My Quern

Worked by A Man

I sow my seeds from one seed grown
through stones I split from off one stone
and scouring circles hour by hour
powder the face of time with flour.

Worked by A Woman

The seeds in spring-time danced and spun;
now through my circles grains of sun,
the seeds of autumn, grind and wheel –
my skirt scatters them into meal.

Lines for My Sundial

At Night

I am the axis of the earth,
my aim night's apex in the north;
and on my face the time, unmarked,
feels its way round me in the dark.

At Noon

The time turns without sand or sound
as my light shadow follows round
the lines of hours one by one
marking the tide-marks of the sun.

For the Old Men of the Shells

When a shell brought her to the shore
her hair was all the clothes she wore
trailing the channels of the sea
through the salt blood that flowed in me.

Now scallops serve for whisky cups,
my spirits empty shells in sups
and all my memories ebb in rhyme
impotent in the face of time.

For the Old Women of the Shells

Round my heels your pleats were spread,
a scalloped neckline framed my head;
then I seamed those pleats with holes
to skim the cream from shallow bowls.

Now wrinkled skin and knotted hand
search where the worms cast and the sand
and sea contest in rut and ridge
to match love's badge of pilgrimage.

The Piano Tuner

Six years in training
his right arm
achieving strength enough
to gently ease a tuning peg;
his ear dividing
cycles of sound
like slips of mica.

Then war;
plotting a submarine
in his mind's ear –
pushing aside the head-phones,
his delicate hearing spared
the perforation of death –
no need for him to rush
to the ship's side to watch
the corpses burst up to the air,
the slug's gut finding a new element,
but he was there.

Now, in the withdrawing-room
he sits, pricking the felt,
the action regulated;
accepting tea only to rest his ear,
he leaves his cup half full,
tightens the strings
and keeps the hammers checked.

On the Arklow Lightship

A sailing ship, complete
with mizzen, gallant, topsail, royal
and all her rigging, cleats and stays,
prow-wave and wake; made on the Arklow lightship,
anchored and wallowing at fifty-two fifty North
by five fifty-eight West.
The man who modelled her must hear
his own discarded beer-cans on calm days
hit the ship's side, and in high winds
have learnt to disregard the kick
of anchor chain and to await
his knife's return, sliding across the desk.

Fixed in a world in which the inaccessible
proximity of objects must have tried
his patience, he must try it more,
accepting in the end his own heart's synonym
stepped in a bottle.

At the Conference

All heads bowed,
the speaker speaks
many words.
On the desks, the handouts,
a refuge from the wind
that dries the brain,
the thirst for knowledge parched
au près de la fontaine.

And yet, without dry lips
there is less pleasure
in the tongue's moisture;
and as the speaker modestly concludes,
there is left behind a taste
in every mind, that makes communion
with consecrated wine.

Quarry

What drew those farmers up
to terrace mountains
to the end of soil?
Providing for their own,
what drew them down
with their immense yoked oxen
pushing back the stone
on the tight angle of descent
to feed the unceasing shuffling
of the marble saws?

They paved the town, furnished
its tables. Now they too
are tumbled down.
Their skills are used
to turn maquettes to stone
for sculptors too old, too busy
to carve out their own
aggrandisement.

         Now, high above
the night-lights of the plain,
old farms stand empty
where the chestnut trees
have rooted up the walls,
destroyed the olives and turned
the grass to mould. Their slow
relentless reclamation has allowed
a last wild pig, mad without mating,
to turn up truffles with his snout.
The hunters hunt him out.

In Antalya

On the steps of the old harbour
an old man sings – I know nothing
of what he sings, save that he sings
for me. His smile, not quite the crescent
of the moon, is warm: his eyes are creased
by light bouncing off white marble,
off ochre-coloured cliffs, dancing
on turquoise seas. He has seen centuries,
peoples come and go, cities in ruins,
cities raised again: but all are held together
by the simple line of his song.
Over and over the same line slightly shifts,
for whatever words he sings.
His singing is older than the muezzin's call to prayer:
it is older than the up-thrust of the mountains:
older than geology. When he sings at night,
the light of the sun smiles in the smile of the moon.
The song is beyond memory. Remember it.

Chocolate

It used to be cocoa.

You mixed the powder with warm milk – a little
stirred and stirred to make a paste
stirred and stirred to make a mug

of cocoa. Not chocolate.

Then you – not anyone else but you –
added the sugar. You still can.
Just buy the right stuff.

OK? Now you sit down and become the ad.

You should be on an old wooden chair
at any kind of table. No, no, no –
get off the couch, this is not about sex.
This is about communion between you
and the mug and the cocoa –
no distractions, please.

All done? – but you forgot the spoon!
Look in! See there – that dark circle round the base?
That's the last mystery. You may stir to eternity,
it will always be there, that sweet and bitter taste.
It would be a shame to miss it, just before night.

Amoretti

For Barbara

I

There was no kind of hunting when we two
sighted each other – perhaps I stared, maybe
you turned your head, and as our bodies drew
together as a mare and stallion free
at last in the one field we nuzzled cheeks
breathing each other's breath; or as the sea
nudging explores its own flood-tide and seeks
new land above familiar marks, and talks
among strange rocks and crevices, or speaks
words of enticement, so did we in walks
along the edge of our own shores – till brave
enough to step where custom baulks
and, as sea-horses playing in a wave,
to prance and tumble in the joy its breaking gave.

II

That winter day my feelings were still numb
as we took time together on the hill,
followed by earnest hungry sheep, whose dumb
demand and shuffling feet in snow were still
behind us after half a mile, while we
laughed winter laughs and chased them back until
they guessed we were of some strange pedigree
anxious to be alone; yet thanks to you
not lonely, as we slithered to a tree
and I then held you so you'd have the view
over my shoulder of the fields below
where, puzzled, the sheep watched our love renew
the teasing innocence of long ago
fooling and kissing in the melting snow.

III

When we were young
we were not afraid
to walk barefoot in wet grass at midnight
stroking our cheeks with bog cotton or the edge of a feather:

but now we do all these things
and use our lips and eyelashes
as well.

When we were young
we would run down hills
till our feet thumped the breath out of us
and our laughter came in gasps:

but now, what with running and laughing and kissing,
we are twice as breathless and when we run
we have each other harnessed round the waist
and our hips touch.

When we were young
we were not afraid
to make nests for ourselves in dead bracken
protected by arches of brambles:
but we did not make love in their shelter
in the spring gales as we do now, and you handle your skirt
with even less modesty than you did as a girl.

I can see the way this is leading us:
you loving me and me loving you
is making us younger than anyone has ever been before
except for Adam and Eve:

But we have the fun
of knowing all about it
and when we pluck figs
we leave the fig leaves on the trees.

IV

Where you sleep now I travel to in mind,
from six miles high fancying we pass your dreams
under our wings in the jet stream of night:
below, spark ribbons leading to a town
that gathers like a galaxy, or the one light
from a ranch attic starring the dark pasture,
tip all my senses over to the ground
gathering dreams from where they might float free
to where you sleep and have reality.

V

I write this poem with a heart of stone,
scratching Ben Sgriol, or a slip of it from
the cairn, having no paper and no pen
but the smooth heart-shaped stone you gave to me
from a long shore an ocean wide away –
which streaks its heart-dust on the mica-schist.
Below green sphagnum, cushioning a spring,
seeps to a lochan on to slake the sea
where – if these stones should slip into the stream
and nudge past pools to where the limbs of land
spread for an estuary – our hearts will be
tumbled and fussed, and all my metaphors
will loosen their old troubles in the waves
of true events shouting and shingling on the shores.

VI

Remember, love, before you blame us both,
the high-bridged stream with fallen trees below
where you, brushing the damp furze from your face
returning sodden from the autumn woods,
the stream a torrent, now fancied its force
uprooting all that wreckage in the hour
we were gone, knowing it was not so.
In other places you have said the tide
might swoop us past the bridge and leave us slack
in dead water, but the sea will turn
this way swooping again and seeming never tired
of its old games, just as among the oaks
we saw a daft November butterfly
still dodging drips and leaving through the damp
a white trail flickering with some mad delight
of nature, natural to all, to us also.

VII

Sometimes I seem a wind about your house
that thumps at gables and through gaps of doors
sneaks in with troubled gusts where a slim mouse
runs furtive between hidey-holes on floors
fanned by a searching draught. Noisy outside,
or silent, but within, I give you cause
to fear turmoil should you at last decide
to air the house when winter might prevail.
But, thrust by a wild element denied
too long till you first loved me in a gale,
and troubling still to pin the leaves you wreathe
round old memorials, you must not quail –
for all the worrying that the winds bequeath
is spent to keep alive the air we breathe.

VIII

I asked what you would like, and when you said
'something I'd made myself and made for you',
daft notions, twitterings of a poem or two,
hopped into sight, cheeky as birds with heads
cock-eyed for bacon rinds and praise: but who
am I to fetch an aviary to your lawn,
who cannot stand the noise now it's near dawn
and one eye open's all that I can do
after a night of study full of yawns
as dumb as a sick budgie – but don't take
my bird-seed from me yet since, for your sake,
I'll chirp a chirrup for when you were born,
and though my gift for song's but half awake,
don't you forget you have the gift of everything I make.

IX

In the brown Kelvin
a duck and drake struggle after rain;
missing the one eddy that curls up to the bank
they hold together
in the ominous ripple of flood water.
But, giving way, she looks down river
as she's swept towards the weir,
so he gives in as well.
Just as I start to fear for them
with white-barred flashes
they both take to air.

And now at night twelve eider –
thirteen – push into the ebb
at Hungerford
while we lean on a granite balustrade
and kiss under a hat and an umbrella's slant.
A distant trumpet busks from the far bank
across reflections,
and the ducks
dip and snuffle in the dark water
billowing with mud.

It should be nothing to us
that these plump feathered preeners
stay afloat – but still, I squeeze
the swell that marks your hip
under the warm fabric of your coat.

X

that time we huddled in the heather hills
so full of laughter as we fought to shield
each the other each from coming rain,
and rolling over on the springing stems
soaked our backs and faces and our
coats got stuck all over with dry pollen grains
and when we had to pluck and each brush down
the other's clothing – such gentle pressure
of your breasts under your coat –

do you remember how our discretion long ago,
seemed innocent of wrong? – and still seems so.

XI

Standing together in the clean night air
you watched the sea – we could just hear
the flood tide lapping – but I watched your hair,
dark, shining, slipped behind your ear
like water on its way round a smooth stone:
you seemed to have been flowing everywhere
in my best dreams – and then that night
how innocently we did not sleep alone
but clung kindly together – do you recall
when you undressed in the soft candlelight
I watched your shadow lapping on the wall?
Next day, not certain this was the real world,
I ran my fingers gently over all
the eddies in the sheets where you had curled.

XII

Now there are no misgivings we can give
and all those others who were drifting by
like mist about the rose in its green hedge
moist and insinuate, try
as they may, cannot evermore allege
it has no blossom save in a clear sky,
or spurn its offering as no true gift
because it's wild: for though we're on the edge
of winter, here's the uncultured day
still coloured by its rose and bees still fly
for fodder in its flowers, and the drift
of all that doubting damp surmise
has passed and leaves us only with the play
of light in ours to give to others' eyes.

XIII

I watched you garden under a dark sky
when cold winter horizontal light
ruffled the crumbled soil and crept round clods
discovering with huge shadows a late fly
or tumbling beetle, busy until night
burying a limp shrew where the brown pods
of broken beans lay flattened in the earth
by piled potato shaws all soft with blight;
and wondered how, in such a sullen time,
you dug tenacious, certain of the worth
of what you did and planting in despite
of all that loss, till the plants climbed
where your love sheltered the young growing part
in the old sheltered garden of the heart.

XIV

We suffer the rose go wild
to straggle in a sky
of north wind
testing past desires.

It has nothing:
nothing to show for itself
but bare sticks –
and a hint of impudence
where hairy shoots
probe through the muddy lawn
to mock mowers.

It is enough: it tells
what each knew in the heart:
that there is more than hope for this old,
much loved, up-start.

XV

It is late autumn and the sea
piles up along the coast:
my small boat, crowded with creels,
tumbles her hull to the gunwale
in fitful glints of sun
shouldered aside
by the dark shadows of waves.

Drifting her in, I see
I cannot land alone:
the strip we cleared
on the wild boulder shore
rumbles with dragged rocks: I prepare
heroics: I shall
jettison the creels and swim,
towing the boat in,
rope between my teeth.

But here you come, unbidden,
down through the steep green bracken
edging brown, past the tarred shed,
straight out into the waves and,
breast-deep in the tide,
take my plunging prow
and guide us round
to face the sea for our return to shore
where I unload a small catch –
which you praise,
stretching the sunlight,
brightening the darker days.

XVI

There need be no sorrow in the thorn: to touch
armour in tenderness is not too close
for comfort: gentle, your acts are such
as can pluck blossom from defensive gorse
till wafts of pollen people hedge and field
knowing no limit as the flower knows
no season and, yellowing all year, yields
kisses in winter, autumn, summer, spring.
Thus, though there's death in all that grows,
and under the sun is no new thing;
for each year that you age and every day
you flower still, and will for me always –
and when you kiss I know, as you touch me,
the lips of time touch an eternity.

XVII

Today is your birthday
and you returning home.
I pick mussels at a low ebb tide
now turning in the shape of the new moon.
My back is bent to the work,
my hands near numb.

Streams from choked culverts
rattle down the track,
tracing fresh ways among the seaweed rocks,
and the wind
batters the sea with mad patterns.

Straightening, I know again
your absence
as a hurt beneath my rib.

Tonight we shall taste and eat
and I shall feel
your long spine, curved beside me:
and above the cool rise
of your shoulders
the nape of your neck
warm
under your autumn hair.

XVIII

Strong as my love is for you, it is hard
to find its best expression:
public and private, I would have the world
acknowledge you, but how? –

no monarch worthy and of statesmen, few
to match your truthfulness:
pomp and splendour wasted on a mind
without pretensions;
title and panegyric useless to
the elemental heart.

Now is my chance.

It was your line caught all the fish –
lythe, mackerel, sillocks –
a boxful in a sunlit hour,
myself your oarsman:
on our voyage home,
in sight of all our neighbours
watching from the crofts above the shore;
I, chucking fish guts in the air
snatched and plunged for,
wings about our ears,
present to you
the ultimate honour:
an accolade of gulls.

XIX

You wear only a rainbow hat of straw
in the tepid water up to your shoulders
warm brown in ripples of sun.

I see you after towelling
on the shadowed path
your rainbow hat, face shaded,
white shirt, shorts, long limbs,
a deer's dappled impression.

On horseback now,
your swatch of hair
switching with flex of flanks,
and the horse's tail – two swathes
of sunlit growth.

Shall you put on your hat before the rain
or in the long grass shake
your loosened mane?

XX

My mind is with you, driving before dawn.
Fearful of hazards, I guess at where you've reached –
the shadows of the Kilbride woods,
where the black cattle merge into the dark;
the steep angled passage high above Loch Carron,
or deer on the long stretch east of Achnasheen:
impatient traffic crossing the Black Isle.

I cannot sleep:
what if harm came to you
and I had not wished you well
for each critical passage of your route?

We are joined not only at the hip
or at the heart; each in the other's care,
sharing, beyond possession,
old passions, gentle, and without demand;
and still you sit upon my knee,
arms round my neck, mine round your waist.
Often we touch or kiss – so whence
this ever-new intimacy, if not from love itself?

This then it is. Quite simple.
The old old story that re-tells itself
beside the hearth; noting the presence
of the household gods,
and far from ready yet
to smash the windscreen of eternity.

XXI

There was an old wall following the crest
with, on the north side, heavy drifts of snow,
tracing past bitter winds. The south was clear,
but for the jumbled stone of that divide,
half buried, broken down. So which was best,
my north, your south, or an exchange, who knows?
and since our independence might appear
like separation to ourselves, we tried
to reach across the wall and sank through crust
heart-deep, and stumbled sometimes, as one must.

But, though fresh snow might sweep the sky
with threatened dark, we still climb high,
touching the lips of light, as mine touched you
on that sharp kissing edge of white and blue.

XXII

I gather in your garden all things green:
chives like a troop of lancers, marjoram,
broad beans purse proud in their fibre down,
tops of broccoli fragile to the touch,
stout courgettes, and the defensive globes
of artichokes hiding their secret hearts;
parsley abundant, and turnips on tip-toe
spurning the soil which nurtured them:

nothing too orderly, for your gentle rule
is in itself obedient to the truth of time;
and the black bramble, always over-bold,
is given leave to search among the stalks.

Flowers there are, nasturtium, marigold,
the yellow cream of the tall meadow-sweet,
sisotheles, bright pink but unashamed;
red poppies dropping petals at the feet
of cardoons princely with their purple flower,
fiery mombretia – and impudent potatoes
out of place.

This sturdy garden on a windswept hill
would never pass for Eden in the world:
but when I stand in it and think of you
who made this happen, then the world is seen
in this small Eden gathering all things green.

XXIII

It is deep winter here, snow on snow;
the mountains in low-angled sun,
their pinks and oranges in late afternoon
glowing above the steel-blue-black
of the inscrutable sea-loch.

The cattle, bracken-orange, snuffle hay,
snow on their backs and snouts; we and they
together, watching how we walk
on the icy snow. We are all
good to each other in our different ways.

And you, born at this time,
what I can give you, that I give:
old love unwavering, companionship,
the gentle habits of the day and night,
good memories, fond thoughts.

It's true there are occasional scuffles,
each one trying to rise
a little higher than the other,
like the chaffinches on the wall
bartering places for the scattered seed,
or the cows pushing and shoving
for some favoured spot
soon seen to be illusory:
and then all settle down.

It is winter, after all, and we are old,
or heading fast that way,
and it is natural to seek the warmth
that you can share with me, as I with you,
this day and every day.

Stornelli

Three Stornelli

All the night long in my dreaming I saw you.
You laughed and smiled and I asked could I kiss you.
You made no reply so I'll answer for you.

I work the vines above her house. I love her.
Her man is thin wine so she'll surely prefer
loving me, when work's done, working above her.

When you turn your back on me pretending pride,
such naked affront shows beauty undenied;
so, front or back, you have no offending side.

Four Stornelli

At spring-flowering-
time we pray to you, oh Blessed Virgin bring
us flowers and, secretly, love's whispering.

Oh summer flower –
Christ's love for man – we pluck you and we cast our
petals and tokens to invoke His power.

Flowers of the fall;
red red autumn and the sword at Eden; all
your tears will never cure, nor your sighs recall.

Flowers of winter;
where you died we mourn the dying of the year
and here The Flower of all men we inter.

Three Echo Stornelli

Love, you're so distant you grieve me   you grieve me
I'll die if you deceive me   you deceive me
Tell me, will you ever believe me?   leave me.

Will you come with me now or will you go?   go
Who? – me or you, or both – or don't you know?   no
Oh please decide – I cannot love you so!   so . . .

Why do you try so hard to wake me?   wake me
You love me no more, so why make me?   make me
Damn you, you purposely mistake me.   take me

Cherry-Tree Poems

I

I amputate your limbs
but in whose arm lies the disease?

You're stealing light you know.
My flowers, my grass, have died
on your account.
Your flowers last
two weeks at most.
Restoring balance,
that's my job;
your roots will compensate,
you will not fall.
I've waited until autumn,
watched your wounds,
taken too little, not too much,
and you must understand
I'm nature too,
monstrous, but natural
unlike you,
whom I have taught conformity.
You should be grateful, for without
this slight curtailment
I'd have been
your executioner.

But when I put the residue
of your offence upon the fire,
you hiss at me.

III

Snow in May, but brief,
and made ridiculous
by the continuing chatter of birds.
It hurries to the ground
as if its life could thereby gain
some small extension,
some image of winter.

The cherry-blossom hangs,
spring-emblem, patiently,
mocked by the tweaking sparrows:
the world of blood
makes its bold gestures now:

but which of you,
snow, flower, or flesh,
is most ephemeral?

VII

A few dead boughs
you've crowded out
with subsequent growth,
and that is all
you have maintained
of your own youth:
I snap them off:
they seem to me as gaunt
and useless as an umbrella frame.

I too have some old branches
without skin and once owned by
a person with my name:
no-one to pluck them out:
deadwood that would proclaim
how picturesque our memories,
old idiot incidents
that make us blush and squirm
for space, while the green worm
chops up our leaves for salad
and we turn yellow in the sun.

VIII

Jointed and skinned, your trunk,
with stump-armed benediction,
seasons under a green elm.
On such a diet half your weight is lost:
my bees have long forgotten you, and I
could stick steel spears
into your starts and checks
and yet do you no hurt.

The wood priest is called in
to gouge his prayers
in your hollow sounds.
He speaks of mysteries,
chiselling; on dry days
with a rasp.

May your priest sing for you.
Body and blood,
these little miracles
take some doing:
it must be hard enough
to be reborn like a pelt glove,
created inside out;
to wake and stretch
within the holy orders of his hands.

IX

Saying good-night to guests;
a light, conventional,
at the door:
regret a tired relief:
turning each cherry blossom
to a Chinese lantern,
a disembodied luminosity,
the stars dimly perceived to be
no more miraculous
than this transfiguration:
and even our good-nights
become a symbol of all friendships
momentarily realised.

Our recognition dulled
by casual fashion,
I omit to kiss her hand,
my wife to offer hers, and,
without bow or curtsy,
we shut the door,
refusing to admit.

X

For Wilma 23.4.75

You and the cherry tree
were born in the same year:
both touched the world with the first start
of knowledge in its place, your cry,
its silence, balancing your forms.

The tree chose this,
your birth day in late spring,
to open its new flowers. So,
as you lean in mutual grace,
I sense you, startled, both reborn.

New World Poems

Nashawena

Here in the New World, still so new to me,
something familiar in the unkept track,
the half-forgotten spring, the smell of sea
or weathered porch – the gentle amity
of friends, considerate; brings welcome back
things I had feared long lost; though, being found
only half credited – as the muffled sound
of a bell-buoy lurching distantly
in fog. But though we're all on shifting ground
this island's rooted in mysterious sand,
as though the amaranth or the untouched tree
of Eden here might grow, as so do we,
discovering in what once was Prospero's land
our own youth catching us by heart and hand.

Naushon

The mist among the green beech leaves,
trees dripping on the sandy track,
the leaves of last year, floating,
bronze, brass, copper, grey and verdigris,
on a dark amber pool.

Above our heads wind spins in tree tops;
ahead, a buck, grazing, raises
his clean-antlered head, his white scut
twitching. Curious, he watches
and then feeds again.

We need not be so relevant,
so be it we tread soft upon this earth,
enjoying anonymity.

The crickets skirr: beetles scurry,
and a monarch butterfly dances overhead
en route for South America.

Nashawena Shoreline

It's a hunt breaking surface
that makes this champagne sea
as, chased by blues, a shoal of whitebait
silvers the sands, gasping to death,
then rescued by a wave, but
certain to beach themselves again.
Mussel shells in millions, cast clean up,
glisten slate blue among torn seaweed fronds
of glutinous shining brown – and there,
across the sand, straight to the water's edge,
recent coyote tracks
show where the hunter headed for the spoil.

Cape Cod Clearing

My mind has drifted somewhere else
rooting among the best-remembered dead:
sweet truffles there beneath the brown leaves;
a rotting book of memory, stanzas impressed
upon each other – it will take
an archaeological dig to analyse this deposition.

The feathery white grasses flow in the evening's sunlit wind,
swaying among the children's graves – those stubby hard stones
planted all too plentiful upon a sandy mound.
Scarlet fever took them all, and so
the old well was abandoned – mere superstition –
and a new one dug.

As the sun pales in the late day's haze
a coyote crosses the path ahead,
sleek nemesis, sliding silent
past the bay-berry, now shedding leaves,
penetrating the impenetrable cat-brier of the mind.

Duck Pond

No ducks. Wrong time of year.
Instead, my good friends, both in blue,
straw-hatted, straight-backed,
elegant in the punt.

Beneath the green beech leaves
of the surrounding woods,
the dead of other years: and there and everywhere
foreshadowed, Autumn stalks the saplings,
camouflaged, his shotgun sloping
from his elbow-crook, with open breach,
ready for the snug fit of the cartridges.

He jerks the breach shut with a click,
and eyes our boat as Charon might
a vessel strayed from Acheron.

Our oars are folded
and our finger-trails feather the water.

Soon it is time to go.
The oarlocks jerk to attention
and the boat slides easy;
eyes steady on the farther shore,
backs to the board-walk.

Ply the oars swiftly now,
and shoot us smoothly
through the narrow barrels of time.

At the Red House

I am surrounded by birds I cannot name:
the chestnut-chested ones, a skilled platoon
spread out and quartering the meadow for grubs,
and in the grass, some small brown inconspicuous bird
goes surely about its business.
The swallows – these I know, fork-tailed
and amorous with the wind:
but from the bushes and the trees,
and from the upper porch and from I know not where
come other voices full of messages – the evening news –
and I have not a word of it and cannot name
a single orator.
                    How ignorant I must seem to them.
Do I not know the need to gather now?
Have I no children? Surely I do not merely feed myself?

From far away, the bell-buoy sounds my funeral,
its lonely toll joining bird-song rebuke
as though such creatures as ourselves
were wasted on the earth.

Penikese

Long after I have left my summer seat
and the ice has melted in the cocktail glass,
the birds still labour for their lives.

Out there by Penikese the sea's benign,
the sand-bar showing green,
the rocks' dark purple warning
clear through the full tide.

It is too far to swim.

The boys keep pigs, set traps for lobsters –
on the menu no more than twice a week
is the unwritten rule:
the island boat is locked.

This is a prison for unruly kids.
Most re-offend; but one
or two slip out of their worst habits.

Visitors are welcome but, unlike the birds
who can enjoy their irreproachable necessities,
we're advised to walk only on the paths -

there's poison ivy everywhere you stray.

On South Bluffs Road

On South Bluffs Road by Vineyard Sound
crickets abound, and the bank swallows
chitter, clearing insects
from the hot bay-berry-scented air.

Granite erratics lumped with feldspar
lurk among the trees where the grey cat-bird
and the chickadee call.
A small woodpecker drills and,
walking through the woods,
my face is stroked by threads
of caterpillar silk and spiders' webs.

A spotted fawn, its mother no doubt dead,
pursues me child-like, with its tongue
feeling its lips in hope of milk;
and, nearly all timidity set aside,
stretches its neck towards my proffered fingers,
sniffs and, at the last second, darts away.

Towards the Western Bluffs

At Tarpaulin Cove a fine two-master
rides at anchor, floating on the fog.

Our own crew, still ashore,
pushes through cat-briar to the graves
of sea captains from Connecticut,
the angel of death presiding over them:
'Died at sea.' 'Died in the thirty-third year
of his age.' – And there a Star of David:
others too, of mariners unnamed,
but no less touching
for the imprecision of their claims.

The air is damp: the throb of engines dulled
in the grey mist clinging to the sea.
A distant foghorn hails the old hazards:
the careless officer of the watch,
the skiff invisible to the radar till too late.

In such a mist, it seems
time's arrow sweeps in circles too,
picking out our graves,
our lives a faint smear
on a monochrome screen,
its gnomon footed in chaos,

and pointing towards
some uncreated star.

At the Top of the Island

I'm at the top of the Island close beside
a huge granite boulder – Merrill's Monument.
'1800-1884' beneath his name, all done in deep-cut lettering.
On its crown, a rounded pillar of rubble and cement
is finished off with pebbles – sperm white
for the tip of Captain Merrill's penis-proud erection.
It's marked on all the charts.

His frank statement stands in the sunlight,
sees the browned bodies of practiced women
sailing by in splendid yachts, their white sails
a surrender to his powers.

On the horizon, No Man's Land,
the navy's island bombed and shelled to bits –
old Merrill's ultimate weapon seeming aimed
at an outpost he would never have destroyed.

Love Poems

Lines for a Wedding Pledge for Marcus and Julie Longmuir

With apologies to Ben Jonson

Drink now, not only with your eyes:
Pledge whisky and not wine.
Kiss not too lightly on the lip;
Though whisky is divine
The thirst that from true love doth rise
Does not to fear incline
Drink deep – it will not do to sip
At such an ancient shrine.

Love's not so light to let it loose
Like spirits to the air
Though angels touch you on the hip
Here is no angels' share,
For you are flesh and you can bruise
Be brave – and yet take care
That on love's quaich is your best grip
To dare what love alone can dare.

No Nightfall in June

No nightfall in June,
only a hot bird-hush –
exhaustion tucked
into a feather bed –
favours abandoned
in the sweet heat of sweat:
the inside of my thigh
slid on the neck
of your two limbs and then
held close, a tense meniscus
of new moons, our surface
drawn up at the sides
like wings, or eyes
half-open, half-asleep.

On the Hill Brow

On the hill brow
the bracken breaks the wind.
We shelter with the rabbit
and observe
the cirrus-clouds.
The private bee
nudges our cheeks;
we pet and play at love,
our hands explore
warm limbs, we wear
two foolish smiles,
and hear the mower
threatening the hay
oh – miles away!

Valentine

You watch me
dress at my window
every morning
you watch me
brush my hair
I won't tell anyone
I promise
if you like
watch me tomorrow
no-one else
sees me like that
only you
cross my heart
it's true.

After-Dinner Grace in Monometers, For Two Only

Take care
to spare
the heart
in part
at least
from priest
and prayer;
and share
the love
that dove
and cross
(they'd toss
a twig
or fig-
leaf on
our fon-
dling fights
these nights)
would claim.

A game
with nak-
ed stakes
is not
for rot-
ten roots
but shoots
and spears.

Though fears
beset
you, yet
please say
we may
succumb –
a crumb
won't feed
the seed

of lust,
and dust
to dust's
a must-
y creed
to feed
upon –
a mon-
ument
to spent
endeav-
ours nev-
er cast
to last.

But see;
I'll be
your priest:
at least
you'll know
that though
you fear
to hear
what's true,
if you
confess
I'll bless
your eyes,
your thighs,
your lips,
your slips
from grace,
embrace
the place
you know
I go
for most.

Oh host-
ess best
divest-
ed, share
this prayer:
and ans-
wering dance
this dance –
and dance,
entrancing, darling dancing dancer,
dance!

Out of Season

Under a grey wild sky wild roses toss
– husk hazel, rattling holly, twitch of birch –
at the broad stepping stones no one can cross
– drowned alder, splitting willow, creak of pine –

and you and I, walking above the cliff
in the wide draught of the Atlantic air,
release our hands to go more safely there
– buzzards are plentiful and rabbits scarce –

so hurry home and coorie by the hearth
– quick birch, hot ash, green elder, steady rowan –
we'll kindle logs when we've stripped off the moss
and save the year, in bed, from total loss.

Valentine

You bet your life and also mine upon it,
that this is not another bleeding sonnet:
for though it's set up the required iamb
and rhymes in couplets sweet as cheapest jam
and puts pentameters in smart array
parading meekly on Love's holiday
and has a THROBBING HEART as centre-piece,
the only way it can achieve that's by
cutting or adding oddities on the sly;
for proper sonnets should have fourteen lines -
an even number which perforce declines
to have a centre – hence this loving stanza
to my heart-throb's a thirteen-lined romanza.

Birthday Poems

For Kirsten MacLeod on Her Fourteenth Birthday

Fourteen's an age for sonneteers and you: –
so, to clean sweep the world we'll make a cloud
out of the grains of dust and count them too
and find if Archimedes has allowed
that gold can dance and dross can settle down –
for where's the joy in judging every crown
by dipping the world's particles in a pan
to measure up the mischief that's in man:
besides, though I shall truly count my lines,
you'll tip fourteen for better measure still
and sweep beyond the folly that confines
my old ideas, intending to fulfil
more hopes than I remember – though I trust
that I will catch their sunlight in the dust.

For Meg Bateman on the Occasion of her Fiftieth Birthday

I search among the trees to find your like:

easy to say the rowan, with bonnie brackets of flowers
and bright fruitfulness: but your place
is not defending gates and graves from spooks.

The fresh green larch in spring with pink-tipped fingers
just might serve, but you were never made to stand in line or,
on your own, be twisted by the wind.

You have nobility – music also –
but I cannot find your likeness in the yew's
dark shade, poisonous to creatures that you love:

and, despite its unmatched green and copper,
never the smooth-barked beech,
below which nothing is allowed to grow.

You are far firmer rooted than the birch,
however delicate and lovely in the spring,
or rich in winter with fine purple twigs;

and, though your roots go deep in knowledge,
I would not claim you for the hazel, too
fitful in fruitfulness and treasured most by mice.

You have the oak's sturdiness, it's true, yet not so
unyielding nor so slow: besides, hunters
of wild pigs in your woods would cause you grief.

The holly, that loves the oak tree's shade,
has far too high a gloss, and its defensive temperament,
tough-skinned and spikey, has no place by your side;

and though, like the red-barked pine, with its high canopy
of deepest green, you move with native right
through the long glens of Alba, yours is a nature far more sensitive.

Like the deep-rooted ash, your feet might rest in the clear stream
or cool lochside, but those thick black-tipped fingers,
as tardy as the oak to feel spring air, were never yours.

Close to its heart, the willow shares with you old mysteries,
and its soft-furred inflorescence reminds me of your love of cats,
but it bears too many sorrows for your turn of mind:

your thoughts are cheerful, your presence fragrant as yellow gorse,
for whom, always in flower, kisses are never out of season;
but, though sturdy in your own defence, I'd never call you prickly.

The blackthorn, with its fairy folk fast in attendance,
or the whitethorn with pink flowers first to form,
these might answer, were they not so sharp.

The pretty gean, so lady-like in spring,
might take your hand, you in a fresh print dress,
but as the cherries on its boughs are bitter-sweet

it will not do. The alder now, I might consider,
with its heart-shaped leaves, for love is ever with you
and your heart knows no concealment – yet there is something

missing as I search among the trees to find your like:

until I turn towards the orchard of your mind
and there at last I see you, unequivocal,
still holding the spring blossom in your eyes,

and yet, already evident, the sweet fruit,
the apple that is formed, joyful and sinless
in the generous heart, the kindness of your soul.

For Ivan Mavor

I've an idea that fourteen lines of verse
make up a sonnet, not a birthday ode,
and, for a young man, should be fresh and terse
or preferably in computer code.
But fourteen years brings fourteen lines to mind
and, since you're learning French and German too
and speak so pleasantly, no doubt you'll find
a little room for English to wish you
a happy birthday – and accept these signs
from the brain's circuitry as a slim clue
to thoughts beyond computing, and designs
broad as affections; though, as my end nears,
I know I'll never fill my fourteen lines
with half the grace as you have filled the years.

Northern Latitudes

Scotland's Thistle

Your spiked leaves drawing blood:
belligerent beauty, wounding the heart:
all to protect a proud purple crown,
that its soft thistle-down may float
in active air, on liberating winds,
to spread the urgent seed
like a free sovereign people growing.

At the Giants' Graves

At the giants' graves an insect alights
upon my marriage finger where I wear no ring,
though married still and, for a moment it seems,
to nature too.

Here, where walked the teachers of Pythagoras,
the stones, selected for ancestral dead,
are now exposed, and the black fly,
and the sweet descending chaffinch-call,
answered among the trees,
tell how we all might transmigrate
in song and whizz of wings.

In Winter

   driving through driving snow
the eye is mesmerised by the flow
of flakes, like migrants in a troubled time
travelling from distant wars. Rime
sticks to the wipers – to and fro
they sway and creak – a tired slow
defensive gesture of an old man's hand
passing through air, too tired to understand.

Clogged, burdened by memory, we know
no cure for our past useless shames;
endless irrelevance creeps in; we stow
facts into snowdrifts, all our claims
smothering. Wind, hard, level, cannot blow
even a gentle hollow in that deep white land:
the war has passed us over; there shall be no
blind prodding with a pole for names
buried beyond devotion.
                   Even so,
a dog, cold-nosed, still snuffles at the snow.

Northern Latitudes

They, whose solstice bears
the urgency of fear
far from the sun,
have they not passed beyond
the civilised assertions
and made their compromise
with all their origins
on tougher rock?
Living on the extremities,
their attentive eyes
focus on distant objects,
universal skies.

Only in stories
or the weather's phrase
remembering kings
and currents of the sea
do they evoke the heroes
summoning tragedy
they tighten their religion,
clean the wells,
and dig fertility
into the ground,
knowing the ice may yet return
and germination die
within the seed.

Iceland Seen from Skye

Between the white rim of the ridge
and the white rim of the sea, a dark territory:
gusts hunting hollows.

A lone redshank piping disconsolate
echoes from the escarpment;
burbles of brown grouse
are muted in wet heather
the ptarmigan grunting among icy rocks.
Below, stream music, turbulent,
as if the unrepeatable lark
sang in the cold-edged winter air
even in dead of night.

Foot-wary, one sees
startling red-rose mosses
in the orange grass;
spaghnum viridian
white wisps of fescue
black moss, moss lime-green,
the glistening rock, and then
a widening light turning west
into the wind:
as the black vapour of approaching hail
streaks in, sea-flattening,
no headgear is secure
eyes weep in the sharp air.

To these elements we are not old or young,
not male or female, nothing now
but the essential thought of life
under criticism from the spinning air
boxing about with tussocks of the bogs,
upturning waterfalls, rattling stones in gullies,
wisping the flowing tails of ponies
standing in sodden ground.

All winter, patient beasts stand patient:
the people also calm on the edges of calamities,
for whom the night-in-day is an old test of nerve,
and the volcanic urge of energies suppressed
is the fine horse they ride in summer nights on sunlit hills
– people who curl down in a thundering wave
of natural pride, but who have swallowed
salt enough to parch the lungs of those
for whom the sea is stranger,
knowing the limits living on that edge.

Old fisherman – the heart-grip of your grin
is a sword of plaited steel
against the anguished memory
of a deck swept clean of men.

- - - - - - - - - - - - - -

Here we come streaming out - Guðmundur
smelling fish-money in the midnight air;
women of startling stature, keen-eyed,
uncompromising judges.

Island history –
in the thin years just one man left to build
the soaring columns of tall Hallgrim's kirk:
or Jón, sea on the surface of his eyes,
silencing his daughters and their guests,
to hear it breathe its music at his door.

Here love of the law's spirit
led to the spear-stabbed abscess
and Njál's blood-stained limp to Þingvellir,
blustering with well-wrought curses
– bitter pilgrimage to see
the world's first parliament traduced:
the land traversed under his injured foot
like his brain by turns on fire
with righteousness, ice-cold with intent.

No rage was ever holier than this
and no defeat more utter and complete –
save that his protest still
brightens the eye of truth
as the keen wind blurs the eye
searching the dark territory
between the white rim of the ridge
the white rim of the sea,
hunting around the bastions to find
the chinks in the defence
of our battling humanity.

Six Composers

Erik Chisholm

You premiered Berlioz and Mozart;
played beside Casella; page-turned for Bartók
and entertained him in your home, the pair of you
sharing pianistic skills and love of your traditions.
You performed Szymanowski for the man himself,
and rescued Walton when he lost the place
in his own music; accompanied Paul Hindemith,
and then played Schmitt to Schmitt.

But you were no outsider, for when you sat beside them,
they sat with you, heard how you played, and
learnt from you, both of your native music and of each other –
for it was you, uniquely, who brought such men together.

Well, you and I have been together now
for several years. As well we never met.
You were so far ahead – besides, we would have fought,
fighting the powers that be, that still
obstruct our shared ideals.

Giving more to others than you ever gave yourself,
you died too young and left your music
lying for years in trunks. Such riches have emerged –
those tiny perfect gems of Scottish airs,
blue as the brightest waters of the lochs;
and the ennobling echoes, as the piobaireachd sounds
'savage and shrill': necklaces of notes
as sensual as the East; crowns of concertos;
operas formed from forbidding myths
and skulls of stark realities;
and works whose craft is in their mysteries,
dark and profound.

Your ashes have been scattered none knows where,
but should there be existence after death, yours would be hunting
through the wild star-scape of universal mind,
chasing a restless muse, that you
might embrace her loveliness once more,
no matter what, if anything, she wore.

Alexander Campbell MacKenzie

Of all this splendid company, you are the one
I wish could ask me out to dinner.
You and old Elgar, and your ladies too –
your oh so pretty wife with that sweet voice,
whom you defended from the family mob
in Edinburgh, thinking they had you jammed
into your poor dead father's shoes.

But we would have your father's ghost
to play *The Nameless Lassie* on his versatile fiddle,
and someone from Sondershausen – perhaps the Duke?
and your old friend Franz Liszt would do a turn,
and some of those peasants who,
at Borgo alla Castello, ceased to sing
because of you, the maestro, composing in the tower
and not to be disturbed. Yes, they would come
and sing their hearts out just for music's sake.

And that fine Scottish lady, Jessie Taylor,
who left Wagner's heart in tatters, and for whom
you wrote that Rhapsody – its centrepiece
based on *She's fair but she's faus'* – she must
have understood, and smiled. We'll have her too
and she will bring the best Chianti.

And then Paderewski – he'll throw caution
to the winds, Poland and Scotland whirling
to your wild way with *The Reel of Tulloch*.
And look, here's Sarasate – he's slipped in
to play your *Pibroch Suite* by memory,
bringing the hills of Scotland there
beside the candle light.
                    And then, at last,
you'll play for us at my request. It's
On the Loch. I know how much nostalgia
rests upon those gentle oars, and I shall drink to you,
my old companion whom I never knew
but know so well, and Elgar too,

your so admiring pupil, remembering
"those spacious days". And when we're done,
we'll all stream out into the street,
singing lewd catches as the clock strikes twelve,
and caper with Sir Andrew Aguecheek,
and Toby Belch, nudge Dickens in the ribs –
and so to bed.

Ghosts, ghosts, ghosts – but, oh,
the music still reshapes the midnight air.

Hamish MacCunn

For Alan Riach

Ay, I was handsome then; John Pettie painted me
as Bonnie Prince Charlie; and then again
as an eighteenth-century beau –
a bonnie lass beside me – holding
the silver boss of a walking stick
just to my lips.

But that's not me. Not me at all.
I can't stand frippery.
I'd sooner bear a claymore,
sharp, to the point:
or be an eagle
spreading my primaries,
soaring on Scotland blue,
crying slogans of the clans
as they deal out triumphs and dooms.

The Lay of the Last Minstrel? –
I saw to it he'd never be the last!
And then that seely Duke and I
brought Diarmid back to life
and played him to the Queen:
and it was I
gave Effie back her lover –
there in Midlothian's Heart –
deep waters welling up,
desires exploding in wordless waves
drowning all modesties.

Music alone can say
the unsayable. That's what I do –
no messing about. This is Scotland.
I am Scots.

When my father's ships
launched out of Greenock

they went on business –
but I saw their beauty too
on the wide Firth of Clyde;
and those sea-lochs long fingered
into the rugged hills round Arrochar;
and in the glens I heard
the multiple songs of streams,
and there, on Arran,
met my love, sweet Alison,
as pretty and as tiny as a bird.
I sang for her and she for me.

And there was just one child,
called up for war.

Goodbye. Goodbye, dear Fergus –
Leave me a dram in crystal by my side –
and light my cigarette.
Cancer leaves no option.
Off you go son, you're safer at the front
than I am here, coughing
beneath the shadow of Cìr Mhòr –
and Slàinte Mhath! Good Health! My glass is full.
The one thing left to do is empty it.

Michael Marra

Are you the fox that dances,
are your eyes headlamps,
that we stay rooted to the spot;
or is it that deep soft purring growl
that charms us into harmonies
no-one could rescue from an irretrievable edge
except yourself?

Gruff old magician, I would not dare
to play in any game with you,
and yet I know that,
now you've joined 'the one big thing',
you'd find a place for all of us
to dance and sing.

.

William Kinloch

Ssshh! It's not safe here. The curtain swells;
a door has opened down the corridor:
whispers of music follow whoever walks
along these carpets of secrets ...
and there you sit,
your fingers are articulating thoughts
that none dare say aloud. The virginals are
your encryption machine – *Susanna Un Jour*?
Yes – She will understand:
the false-accused, those lying elders
Knox and Goodman – She will hear and know
an ally plays for her.

And now, *The Battel of Pavie*. Who won?
It seems so simple – Charles and the Pope:
the French King captured,
and that Scottish Prince so beautiful
laid out upon cold stone
candles surrounding him:
so why on God's earth
did you sing that victory song, and celebrate
wild Spaniards with their arquebusses
bringing down the pride of the French chivalry,
on their caparisoned steeds, their lances falling
"like a field of sugar-cane in a storm"?
Thus, the Spanish priest who saw it all,
describing first a fashion parade
so soon redressed in blood.
Uccello also saw such scenes, but not
such slaughter, not at the hands
of vulgar soldiers, each with his personal
firearm: they tore at the King's clothes
for souvenirs. They would have stripped him naked
had not their own commanders called a halt.

But what was in that victory for a Scot?
Don't tell me you still hoped
for Spanish aid to liberate your Queen?

Was that it? Yet another plot?
Your friend James Lauder sent you to her
with "your daggers and your knives" –
was all your virtuosity given
to covering up a deeper meaning
and hidden weaponry?

You and William Byrd – you must
have known each other. The old recusant
always forgiven by that stark Virgin Queen –
a saving grace in her; but jealousy
overcame her in the end. What was it like
to have been loved as Mary was,
to feel hot flesh within you, to give birth,
to dance so well and play the lute
so finely, to have learnt poetry
from Ronsard and to write,
if not like him, at least with genuine merit
in your native French?

Well, Mary must have suited you, Kinloch.
You both had style. Your *Long Pavan*,
your *Galliard*, your *Fantasie* and your *Ground*
based on *The Huntis Up* - an aubade
for a hunting hunted Queen.

They did not hunt you down,
and I've been on your trail for twenty years
and still have found no proof that would convict –
not that I wish to. I would sooner
watch closely as your fingers race
over the neat virginal keys: you,
like a trickster at a fair,
performing little miracles I cannot quite explain
tangling up history in a crazy interplay of notes,
half-meanings, hints.

No, I am glad that vile spy-master
Walsingham never found you out,
though he got close – Gree's Inn,
the Lauders, father and son. Oh yes, he knew
that much. Or did old William Byrd
pull that one sympathetic string
that still could resonate in Elizabeth's heart
and get her to call off the hunt for you
for love of your wild music?

All in vain for Mary, anyhow:
the last she heard, the sound of her own neck
hacked by the ill-aimed axe.

John Blackwood McEwen

How shall I write of you, the subtlest of them all
with your intelligent gaze, pince-nez perched
upon a prominent nose, your mouth,
without severity, calm under a modest moustache?

Your collar is unbuttoned, a cravat
tucked neatly behind broad lapels,
and your receding hair reveals attentive ears.

You and that half-Scot, Satie
might have made a pair –
two lyric philosophers,
your busy motorboat, *La Rosière*,
rivalling his *Voiles*;
and jaunty, winning *La Racleuse* who
maybe shared with you
a cockle shell at Cap Feret?
Satie would have loved her too.

What was it broke your heart?
The War? Those *Hills o' Heather*
left so far behind, *Where the Wild Thyme Blows*?
The War again?

So much is unrevealed, or said
so quietly
from the quiet of the dead.

Family Poems

Family

Your sister's ill.
No, you can't see her yet,
what shall we get
to cheer her up? A book?
Was it insight made you choose
Three Little Pigs – a home
to outwit death?
We said it made her smile
and happiness suffused
your face. But this was lies.
How could we tell you
that she did not see
or hear or recognise?

But when we tucked you in
your heart burst in your eyes
as though you knew
and would not sleep alone.

So we three lay at night
each touching each
to keep the circle closed,
disown the gap,
as though admission
might concede defeat
and hell skirl in our midst.

Sarah

My little girl
dances like a doll;
when she looks up
her smile's immediate
and fixed, her fingers
on her hem, she skirts
oblivion with formal care
follows the patterns on the floor
knowing the earth may open up
should she tap-touch
the secret lever
on the swivelling slab.

Three months ago
she threshed in straps,
her eyes turned to her brain,
her body crushed,
tubes to each orifice;
the ventilator's sac
gasped like a gill
behind the glass
and in the tent
enriched humidity
and heady air
nurtured her life's import
in this new atmosphere,
the world an alien
environment at odds.

My little girl
dances like a doll,
stasis and movement
featured in her limbs
and in her mind who knows
what ritual purge
to dance death down
below the house,
permit the secret smile.

Interior

My room is decked with skulls:
an old ram jutting from the wall
without opponent; a cow that fell
to a rough rock shore;
a little goat that died in Italy
bearing her first kid.

My room is decked with green:
the fossil antlers of an elk festooned
with ivy; the mirror ivied – by the wall
a slender upstart tree
and grey Atlantic seal, baring his teeth,
a sprout of holly prospering in his snout.

Sound-sensitive is my room –
to hissing logs and hiss of pressure lamp,
or old cracked cello's sudden groan inside its case,
or my tempestuous daughter fluting air
for goats to dance to.

My room has its disturbances and fears:
the gannet's beak that I could never close;
the tiny theatre, ivy-overgrown;
the minute scream from some strange agony
far inside the fire.

This is Christmas eve. We sit alone.
The candles, tinsel, jigsaw half-undone.
Later, I watched her torch-beam on the moor
dart to a neighbour's, but from time to time
point back to pick me out – my arms outstretched
behind the gate to give a reassurance, held
only for its own sake – as it must be,
since there's such scant assurance in reality.

Pattern of Waves

We lie on sand; your wrist across my eyes
filters the sun in soft-hair-rainbows,
and beyond, the children, silhouetted,
leap and flit against the sea
like dancing letters, in and out of words,
their gestures punctuated by the curls
of waves driving them to and fro
with knots and sanderlings. It seems
that they have knit themselves
into the pattern of waves, and laughing,
dancing through our wedding rings,
like a fine shawl, slip from our ties
of love, proclaiming pledges of their own
in semaphore to the sun.

Bathing (from *Six Sea Poems* by Sean Purser)

III

Bathing

On a soft shelving sandbank, to his waist in the water,
A child leaps delighted with dolphinish gasps.

His body and limbs, caressed by the liquid,
Are a world in themselves of warmth and delight.

Brightness like lightning beside him flashes
A hoop of silver circling him round.

Ducking down under, he rises and throws up
Sparks and sparkles into the air,

Till splintering sun-streaks fall down in a shower,
Himself in the midst shaking them off.

He shakes them off, and the memory, with them,
Flashing, outflashes its death in time.

Farmer

In memory of my uncle Travers Nuttall

The clouds careered above the trees,
grass and bog-cotton,
streamered by the wind,
reached towards the fence-
barbs, tagged with wool.
And though well wrapped with hymns
and seeing tears on only those who cared,
the ones I envied leant outside
against the church, for lack of room,
and watched the wind scattering birds,
staining the stones with rain.

At last doors opened
and our shoulders steered
your coffin through the gale:
but as we dropped you into shelter
we sensed you torn away:
the late spring, clean of conscience,
the earth turned.

Bray Head

There has been heather burn;
charred stalks powder shoes
with black and white ash,
nostrils sniff
memories of fire.

Here the dried mud rut
halted the flames
and in the centre of the seaward track
a green ridge runs uninjured
sweet and fresh.

Beyond, the cliffs lift up
the sound of seagulls;
the airflow, moist and salt
entices to the edge where
between elements
delight giddies about.

Returning home
a sudden glance
by the burnt verge
lights on a form
familiar and yet strange:

a frog
an inch from freedom
scorched by a lick of flame
into a black memorial
of its last frantic leap,
is caught half air-borne
on the charcoal stems.

With this trophy for my nephew
delicately pocketed
I wonder when and how it was
that pity, with searing brand-mark,
shrivelled half my heart.

Domestic Interior

The mezza-luna chops in the shallow wooden bowl.
Now and again a walnut leaps to freedom,
as a fine flour forms around the rim.
Crushed garlic, sea salt and green olive oil
are blended in with an old wooden spoon.
The sun has bleached her hair and her hazel eyes
smile gently, as she offers him a taste
of the aïllade poised on a celery stick.

For my Daughter in Black

Out of what shadow will she step
unrecognised?

When her feet scuff the scarfed timber stage
may they feel
cushions of wild thyme,
cool water from Drinan well:
may the salt sweat in her eyes
be from the nudge of a wave,
her black leotard
a sealskin.

May she know at that time
nothing of herself,
wholly other:

even so,
let her be as loved
for what she truly is
as what may be

that she may know
to whom
with whom
she has come home.

For my Son who Would Wear Motley

Not parti-coloured
I suppose - though
in that well-chested
almost breast-plated
heart of yours

march armies
led by white and gold
standards.
But there's no currency
in that exchange,
though you might have it so.

Wear what is yours of old:
a truce, twice signed,
on two sides of one cloth
of gold shot through with white,
white shot with gold.

For Judith Caughie

One of but few who've forced me to concede
in argument, you have been
even-handed, generous, full of fun.
You've kept no secrets, honest with yourself
and others. Handy too: you've shown
what work is, but will not bow the knee
to mere convention.

Artist, teacher, yet you know the earth and sea
are real; harder than marks on paper
which you honour too.

In youth I little thought that I would have
two daughters, but as the years went by
I learnt that blood and water are subservient
to the heart's truth. This you have taught me.

So, on your birthday, bonnie lass,
may all you've given give to you
such happiness.

For Judith and Simon Sweeney 15.10.11

It was always going to be an adventure.
from where you were to where you are today
is quite a distance – but the best journeys
take their time – take chances too. But now
this autumn wedding by the shore
when cattle come home to the crofts,
when the last migrations have flown
and the remaining birdsong comes from faithful friends
who stick it out through winter – robin and wren
with their short and sharp sweet sentences -
your love is witnessed not alone by us,
but by the land and sea – the weather too,
its restless certainty the evidence of life
vigorous, winds full of desires,
rain ready to wash away the dull dust
of static conventions. So you two
belong by nature in this kind of place
and, to our blessings on you both,
it gives its own wild embrace.

For my Grandson Thomas Sean Gormley

Tight fist in mouth,
finger in eye, finding
where each part fits,
you crease your face and cry
the cry of seagulls;
your feet kick air, asking
"are we not meant to fly?"

Voices swim in your ears
a babble of baby clothes,
the ritual gifts.

Little king, you are still free
to cry out as you will,
to claim your claims,
your stretched arm a sceptre,
your head an orb, crowned
with the pulse of thought.

And for His Mother, my Daughter Sarah

So high a tide that brought you to the full,
lifting your little vessel till he swam
and kicked against your harbour walls
and hiccoughed on the brine, in search of air.

And now you've cut his mooring rope
that he may sail far far and wide, yet always know
your harbour as his own.
                        His father, handsome pilot
sure of hand, sails from the same port, knows
the rocks and shoals beyond its sweet embrace.

Always they will return – at dawn and sunset, nightfall,
at all times certain of your love, your heart a compass –
its welcome reckoning the beauty of your smile.

You too were once cut loose, but still return
to your home shores; and then we dance
on sparkling waters, and our fond eyes drink light.

For Paul Gormley

How calm you lie, your cheek
soft settled below her collar bone,
the drum-beat in the womb

heard in its ocean clarity
now through a wall of ribs
distanced and yet the same.

How soft your head, assured its home,
in this new element of air
feeding the darkened ward.

Your wakening can wait:
this time, this meeting
perfectly fulfilled,

your young heart at its work
infusing all your flesh
with the ancestral blood.

Bird Poems

Phalacrocorax Aristotelis (The Shag, or Skart)

The whole day long your liberty,
what wisdom has your leisure brought to mind –
the obverse of our white inconstancy? We,
free as seagulls, squabble on ledges
for your choked-up bones; you swallow stones
for ballast – black submarines, chasing
the streak of nervous fins.
On your long low flight-paths
crossing moon-silver rubbings on the sea,
dark as Diana's nightmares,
do our black secret thoughts
travel with you, anonymous hunters?
Or, as you hang your wings out,
preen the oil and lice
among your flights, and dry
your plumage with a slow bat flap;
do your bald brain-pans, vacant in idiocy,
take pleasure like poor senile men
in the salt dribbling from internal nares
and beak, onto your feet?
But in the sun your bodies
iridesce, your arched necks oily
rainbow negatives: and there is something
in those small round eyes that tells
skart harbour knowledge of a different kind,
more terrible than we could dream of or control;
those silent colonies a cipher
for a hell beyond the hunt, to warn
of devastation, should we try
to fire the fleet of your philosophy.

Adolescent

On this reef
round which the sea worries itself
trying it out from every angle
circling:
a large down-breasted adolescent
cormorant
looks quizzical and squawks.
His ancestors are older than Orion:
of this he is blissfully unaware.

He jets a stream of whitewash excrement
into the western ocean
and dives in.

Champion

My eye is in.
Six birds with seven shots –
calm seas of course, and they are young
and ignorant of the gun;

and now another – no –
he dived too fast.

I know where he will rise and
sure enough I have him almost in the sights.
He dives again.
Time after time I can anticipate
exactly where he'll break the surface.
Pursuing, speeding, slowing, well I know his mind

but he knows mine.

With endurance unimaginable
he scarcely surfaces to breathe,
his lungs and heart
are prodigies of power
his eyes alert
although they should be dimmed
with the near-suffocation of this hunt.

Two shots he's cost me
shots he must have heard
spatter the surface of the sea
just above his arching dive.
A third miss counts me out.
He's up again. More quickly now, tiring,
but still game.

I down the gun and stand up in the boat
according him a boxer's clenched salute.

He knows he's won,
paddling about cocksure,
but is too proud to turn.

Champion of champions,
who is he to care
for the applause of amateurs?

When he goes hunting he catches fish so fast
they're jumping in his gullet.
Never dead until they reach his stomach,
he's yet to choose one that he did not eat.

Snow Bunting

Beyond all hope of life you are alive,
your bell-like calls claiming
a wide plateau of snow and rock and ice,
where I, so alien, am mere fantasy
beside your intimate domestic ways:

guard the heart carefully; the air
is pure and giddy: here it may be
Snow White was laid in her crystal coffin, cold
and inviolate, yet sustained by love:

nor have I summer hopes
to ease the ice, but, like these birds
must nestle with my thoughts
among the scree and love things as they are

for ever, if need be: then, without fear
her throat will yield, and all my words
will, like snow bunting, find a home
in desolate places where no one
should be alone.

The Swift

Deceived by window glass, you beat
the clean arc of your wings against the sash:
your partners flicker, drift and wheel
under the eaves. At human touch
most birds will cower and squeak –
you scream at me, tearing skin with beak.

Your outrage breaks the prison of my will
and, empty-handed, I'm left captive here,
my indecision mocked, my dull days blank,
standing in a portion of the sky
stolen from you to house my jealousy.

A Message to Hirini Melbourne

Hirini,
          the bird-call of your name
was too soon cut in stone, your song
pressed into plastic, and your voice box
buried there, under a heap of ruffled soil
beside the family farm: and just beyond,
the bush, bird-rich and beckoning:-
it is your voice I hear in every call,
bell-like or chattering; a brief alarm,
or doting chuckle as a saddle-back
feeds its mate: at night a kiwi,
stalking grubs; by day the weka
scavenging: or is it you,
antipodean robin, with soft white breast
that comes, familiar, to my feet
to see what I've turned up? –
or there, a sudden fan-tail flash
in tree-fern tops, sweet chattering.

Your voice in all of these,
how shall I return your call
two continents away?
Shall I send terns to scream into your ear
in protest at your death,
or owls, old ladies of the night,
to haunt the spirit world with hoots
to draw you out of hiding?

I could engage a lark to thrill your mind,
a chaffinch to endear you to domestic thoughts;
perhaps a wren with sweet shrill cry
to tease you into search
of your competitor in concealment:
that I might see once more that winning smile,
or catch the way you brushed the air
with your pursed mouth, your putorino
drawing me across oceans of life and death:

hirini,
        hirini,
                hirini,
I send you my song calling from the shore,
pilililiu,
        pilililiu,
                pilililiu:
and when I wake into that other world
where bird-song breathes eternity, we'll sing
hipiriliu,
        piriniliu,
                ripiniliu.

Skylark

who can unstitch a stretch of sky
and with the same song seam it up again,
or tirl the air and needle into notes
a trillion tiny ear-drum taps
with threaded light that makes my eyes,
hereditary, sneeze, and turn to ground
among the labouring insects
beetling balls of dung?

When you fly free and I'm left cutting peat
against a winter half a year away,
remembering at the end of Eden man
was given what would root him to the spot –
a spancelling spade –
I raise my hat and yield the gods a grin
as proof that all creation's crazy made.

It is Dusk

It is dusk as I step out from the porch.
Across the stream on Ruairidh's brae
our black Rose, Highland-Aberdeen-Angus cross,
stands stock still and listening,
her head slightly inclined to her right, her ears alert
to the sweet evening call of a blackbird.
She does not move one bit of her.
She listens. The other cattle graze.
They are closer to me; not of her company.
I too stand still and listen.
What is this magic; this astonishing beauty
apparently without cause?

I speak so softly I hardly hear myself,
 just to say, in Gaelic,
"It is beautiful, isn't it?"
And even at this distance,
Rose hears and knows my voice
and turns her head briefly to acknowledge me.
And all the while the blackbird
sings on in virtuosic clarity
as the light dims and we are all subsumed
into the gentle silence of the night.

Poems and Dialogues Concerning Natural Religion

Jehovah's Witness on Skye

We discuss Noah.
It is June.
Hot days.
The wind speaks only through the bees.
The sea maintains
good-humoured silence.

That old Flood, I say:
his raven eating the eyes
perched on the bloated belly
of a long-drowned child -
what kind of god ordains
such things?

There were warnings, he says.

– For intelligent babies?

– The sins of the fathers.

I throw the book at him,
this earnest Englishman,
his little son
with thumb secure in mouth.

– Onan v. God. God says:
better to fertilise
your brother's barren wife
than masturbate.
And then there's Lot,
raped by his daughters:
father-grand-father
to the tribe, chosen no doubt
and sacred in the rut.

Even the cuckoo
has shut up. As for the sheep
they are kept awake

only by maggots –
the ordered world:
God's itch in the fundament.

Useful, he says.

The useful sun?
swelling the grapes of wrath
for God to trample on? No no.

Let us be brambles
tangling sheep's wool
ripening our berries -
for the fun.

He hears me well; and now
we shift our ground
to the next testament.

- The innocent fig tree
sterilised:
the whip in the temple
where men had traded
for a thousand years.
Just petulance, I say.

The Gadarene swine:
I forgot the Gadarene swine:
God's ordered world again –
this time the maggot in the brain.

We could map the clouds today
they stay so still –

God's Judgement Day to come?

Here is my creed:
all things of beauty;
the whole living lot;

t
ake no more heed.
Take no tomorrow heed
again or ever.

King David's one hundred
and thirty-eighth psalm, he says.

I ask. When I am old
can I "gat heat" as he?
Is there a fair maid left in Israel?
Who then forsook
the work of his own hands?

We part smiling
but gave his child no chance
for one short word.

I had biscuits. No apples.
Biscuits would have done.

Columba to God

I have tried to know suffering as the birds must know it
to hunger with the starved buzzard
to bruise as a battered redwing stupified by storms
to share the cackling fears of the red heathercock.
I am no dove.

My pride has fed on corpses
stabbing the eye of knowledge
a raven pecking at meanings
wanting possession of dead things.

My pens were tugged from the wings of geese
hissing their innocence,
the skins of hollies stripped and boiled
and insects crushed for ink.
Over five hundred calves have crumpled to their knees
to yield pelts for my library of books.

Oh my God forgive! Forgive me – count my ribs –
I too have yielded one for Eves I never touched,
mine a princely negation
– through my coarse cloak they leave
their imprint on the strand –
I would have truly starved
but my kind acolyte slipped milk into my meal.

My only purity in song, I gladly sing.
My one sorrow in dying
to leave others sorrowing.

Columba to King David

You must have written more.
Three fifties?
I myself have covered more vellum than you papyrus.
No poet of your stature writes without foresight.
You saw Christ crowning innocence,
the dove over Jordan, water turned to wine –
and that head on silver in its sauce of blood.

Those poems, where have they all gone?
What stopped your prophecy,
strangled the duty of a bard?
Where was Isaiah if not here and now
before and after – ever with the truth?
What clogged your bowels?
Kingship?

Power and lust and at the latter end – unable.
Yet the Lord shall shepherd you,
great poet that you were.
His sheepflock sing your every surviving word
through matins, lauds and vespers,
decades, centuries, a *laus perennis*.

Your harp? Had you but known –
your little lyre, was it as sweet
as the *tiompan*?

I too have cast my voice
beyond our mortalities.
Has anybody heard?

God give me grace that I may sing
in the same congregation
as you and the Cherubim.

Columba and Saint Finnian

roo-coo-coo
        cu
roo-coo-cu
       roo-coo-cu

Columba, Columbine
you won your war
then spoke peace
but
little dove of Scotland
to those who lost
what have you to say?

roo-coo-coo
        cu
roo-coo-cu
       roo-coo-cu

roo-coo-cu

Saint Brigid to Christ

Lay your cheek bone to mine
let me
nuzzle your shoulder
face me
that I may see
kindness tinge your eyes
be all of you in touch
all visible
knowing all of me

oh – were I in your company –
that is how I
would be with you
my Christ

to cling close at times sorrowful

and on pet days
together
giggle with delight.

Ranging

See how the bells are set, their heads up,
tongues in cheeks – a silent innocence
poised between prime and evensong.
They lurk here among ladders, beams
and stocks, with power and space enough
to claim your life. One touch and this calm
balance will up-end; ton after ton
of alloy – copper, tin: and iron clappers
will applaud your folly with abuse
to knock you from your metaphysical perch.
See how they're placed – ordered
into disorder, in the fear
of a conspiracy to split the steeple.
It happened once. The bells set up a
swing that bridged the belfry
with a note of such agreement
that the thought of man could
hold the stone together for no more
than half an hour. Watch your foot –
from top to bottom of this shuttered nest
out-falls the octave – you could bring
the town into the streets, reset
the clocks. See this inscription:
'Here goes my brave boys!' –
that other one's for death.
Massive: immutable. Man, woman, child; each
an allowance to release their souls:
Look down. You see each sally hangs
from a wheel of fortune: we play games
with magic numbers – caters,
bob and peal, royal and maximus.
You say they shout of laughter;
joy and love? When I'm alone
I clamber through these bells
and hear them cry to God – silent,
vibrant, intense. I tell you
they have primed eternity
to hunt us down.
They have us in their minds.

The Translator Confesses to the Book of Books

I pick my words. I keep them scrupulous, clean
and comprehensible. But this sharp key
that feels for intimacy, truth, The Word,
has turned the fallen tumblers further down;
all your untidy chronicles, your petty crimes,
your tent-pegs and your figs black-blasted, sterile,
make their mark on me. So, blunted stump
and steps, we're both corrupt; defeat
rattling a padlock at the gate, calling
someone to come and help devise
the words to fit the wards of paradise.

Homage to David Hume

Did our perceptions either inhere in something simple and individual, or did the mind perceive some real connection among them, there would be no difficulty in the case. A Treatise Of Human Nature – Appendix.

When memory becomes an empty husk,
a silly hope planted beside a grave;
our persons bundled straw, rakings at dusk,
disordering the life we thought they gave:
when we procure perceptions like a whore
from all the strands of living and of death,
and spill the seed, as Onan's, on the floor
of the world's granary, and breathe our breath
to winnow out the wastes: when we thus blight
all love's proud cause, denying its effect;
we cheat ourselves to find a brief delight
in this small form that struggles to reject
the flail and thresher – as we bind up tight
the sheaves of our creation in your gathering night.

One Irishman to Another

Ah, Bishop Berkeley, 'twill do you no harm
spilling beer on your Vision while raising my arm
to stifle a yawn – 'twas the hop, not the leap
of your tough mental games, that put me to sleep.
Now, if I get you right, I imagine the beer –
or put it this way, the beer's an idea
in my head – I agree – but if it was here
before it was there in the glass I'm not clear
as to how it has passed from my thought to my pleasure
without catalysts like some malt and that treasure
of flowers, the hop – though I tell you bell heather
will certainly do just as well: what a blether
you are Bishop Berkeley – I'm sure that the port
or tar-water you drank did just as it ought
to and if, Bishop Berkeley, 'tis all in my head
not Berkeley but beer'll blur my Vision instead.

The View from October Hills

*And God said, 'Let the earth bring forth the living creature after his
kind.'*

I'm gazing south,
October's on the hills
in brown and gold, descending.
A young stag with single hind
has left the smell of rut
honouring the air. I see him
head high and russet neck
bright eye and blackening bracken mane:
his antler arcs embrace blue skies.

In a fork of rowan on the basalt cliffs
a black raven and her life-long love
reared their bald chick, tender among storms.
Taking my shadow for a parent,
a blind baby croak, cradled,
betrayed the tattered nest.

That sound, for all its misplaced trust,
is sweeter to me now
than the call of my own kind
seeking forgiveness for irreparable crimes:
and my mind's ear is listening on Blaven
to a raven's wing rippling the air
then dipping, so its feathers utter notes.

Long years ago my father
took me where frogs were mating.
I, a little boy, not knowing
what this had to do with me, but laughing
as they kept on falling off.

Male and female created he them
'and man in our image after our likeness.'
So He said.

In whose image then am I, stag, raven, frog?
or, God forbid, the image of that pair
whose murdering lust
putrifies in the court-room:
and if like them, worse still to know
that God's like them also.

The Hot Coal of Truth

The prophet Isaiah was purged of sin by a hot coal on the lips.

And God said many things:
"Let there be Heaven and Earth.
Let there be Hell.
Let there be Death in essence infantile
eating the marrow
of my young."

The boy
pitched through a windscreen;
scarred from cheek to chin,
two smiles – for each side of
the slashed dip
in his lips.

God said:
"Mankind will learn.
The seared mouth,
printed and purified with this truth,
will speak for Me and prophesy
from a crashed mind racked by nightmares."

Man said:
"To Hell with God, to Hell with Him:
what He dreamt up
let Him dwell therein."

The Poet to Plato

The light is in the mind
not in the shadow or the outer world.
You, who could not see in the dark
but sought out the ideal
in worlds beyond your comprehension,
heard no sound – and your impatient eyes
were undilated slits in the revealing night.
Nor did you hear the slight exhale of breath
through the wild pig's nostrils, and the gentle grunt
that claimed a passage across the path
that you could not discern through the dark trees.
You did not wait for his obedient herd,
their sharp hooves pattering on the dirt.
Lucky for you they took you for a fool
and not an enemy.

Come with me now, that you may find
the forgotten wisdom of Pan, the world where Orpheus
subdued the King of Death; that we may hear
the resonance of the cave ring in our thoughts,
uncluttered by the slight incidence of light
on all the paraphernalia of the outer world;
that we may sing the mystery of the night
and learn to honour the Athenian owl;
wintering, wide-eyed, in the cosmic dark.

Ballade for the Duke of Orléans

It was your gates, not fearful, nor too proud,
that opened to new hope against despair,
to that sweet maid who, high above the crowd,
bore in bright armour and with banners fair
her nation's heart, and won with courage rare
your right, where others ruled, to rule again:
given such history, dare you declare
"Je meurs de soif auprès de la fontaine"?

And he who turned that great mediaeval key -
Bishop Kirkmichael, Scot - thus paved the way
through Orléans' gate for marching liberty,
with Scottish captains leading on the day
their tartan troops beside few French; and gay
was Joan of Arc's heart, free of French disdain:
Oh Duke, at that great moment did she say
"Je meurs de soif auprès de la fontaine"?

For suffering to perfection's no true aim:
and poets who toy with suffering are the same
as cheating hearts to whom true love's fair game,
its death passed cheaply off – another's blame.
But knowing this, no poets worth the name,
not now, not ever, should again profane
their maker's art, by claiming what you claim -
"Je meurs de soif auprès de la fontaine".

ENVOI

And, Richard Wilbur, this to you I say:-
we men, and women, were not born for pain:
our loves, our joys again, again gainsay
"Je meurs de soif auprès de la fontaine",
asserting over all your studied woe
(while hearing well your Anglicised refrain)
that from despair hope finds a way to grow
and need not thirst auprès de la fontaine.

Mummified Nun

Closed eyelids her armorial crest,
her hair unbound, a cross is pressed
in her fingers, crossed across her chest.

Her face is creased like seaweed dried,
her belly sunken, wind and tide
leave her untouched and those full wide
breasts are spread out thin:

and written on the parchment of her skin
her fingerprint survives, the last particular,
but unidentified.

Money and title must have made
this tomb. Her whole life gainsaid
by these preserving airs. She paid

in kind, not to evade the crow's
derision or the first dull blows
of earth upon her chest. Who knows
what end she had in mind,

if end at all, – confessions of a kind
more intimate than this sad show of flesh
in atmospheres windless and rarified.

Léborcham to Conchobar

She is too much alone
that girl
her cheeks are pale
with inexplicable desire
then hectic with shame.

I have put her in a darkened room
sap throbs in her head
cramps waste her womb
I have strewn meadowsweet
infused it in honeyed water from
the Drinan spring
but she drinks none.

She will bleed soon.

This winter was too mild
now we are maddened by midges and
though she is sick
milking must still be done
I can just kneel to reach
but my knotted hands are slow
to ease the swollen udder
black flies torment us.

It is pointless
this imprisonment
hers was sorrow from the start
and you old man
old king what do I care
all you would do is
open her young wound
and scar her where her flesh
might for a passing youth
un-shamed uninjured
briefly bloom.

Note: Léborcham was nurse to Deirdre whom she was to rear in isolation until she was of age to marry King Conchobar.

Gráinne to Diarmait

Cast no more unbroken bread;
since he put his arms around me,
his hands pressed to my stomach,
since I thrust your knife into your own thigh
and you made me withdraw it to my shame,
let our token tomorrow be scattered crumbs,
crushed husks, the milled grain:
I have needed you beyond bearing;
as blood flowers in snowflakes I am torn
by the red rose and the white rose of your flesh.

Note: Unbroken bread was left as a sign of chastity to the lovers'
pursuers. It took the embrace of a stranger to break that resolve.

Botticelli to Venus

This is our second childhood – not that age
has played the fool with us, but we have played
with the delight of children who engage
delight with neither fear nor loss. We've made
fools of dials and calendars, held court
in the long grass, the scythe and spade
have not troubled us, it's been our sport
to geld old Time and drop his genitals, maimed,
into the sea –
        and look, I see you step
naked ashore; frank, touching, unashamed,
fresh from the scallop in the willow skep
through whose old uprights of despair and rage
I've woven hope, so men might catch and sow
the seeds of oceans – but where people grow.

The Deeps (from *Six Sea Poems* by Sean Purser)

VI

The Deeps

Down there is darkness such as never
Was on the surface of the earth,
And gulfs steeper than the steepest cliff-falls
Among the most giddying mountain heights.

Red clay and blue mud line its crevasses,
And millions and millions of little shells,
The remains of little lives, extinguished,
Forgotten as if they had never been.

Fittingly the sea is a symbol of eternity,
Where things are lost to sight, and inaccessible
To thought. There even the relics
Of humanity can be but a sparse scattering.

And of what value to itself or another
Is the huge immovable creature
Lying at the very bottom of the ocean, and waving
A faint luminosity to attract its prey?

Three Stone Boats

For Will MacLean

This is a stone boat.
Its name is Will.
Its cargo is Affection,
which Duns Scotus would call Love.
This boat is a ferry,
plying between Applecross and Ashaig.
Sitting on the cargo in the stone boat
is Saint Maelrubha.
He tried to purchase an ordinary wooden boat,
but none of the shipwrights would let him have one.

'We know what these saints do with our boats.
They go out into the Atlantic and are never heard of again.
Or they come back with crazy tales of the Land of Youth,
birds singing psalms, lighting fires on the backs of whales,
and fireballs boiling the sea which has frozen into ice.'

So Maelrubha, like many of his fellow saints,
had to make do with stone.

This particular stone comes from Strath in the Isle of Skye.
It is green marble above, and grey marble below,
where the hull meets the sea.
It has a pink nose and a pink sail,
both of marble from who knows where.

Will is the name of this boat,
because, for all that being a ferry
between Applecross and Ashaig,
is a short and repetitive business,
Will has had the Freedom of choice
to choose it.

If you wish to sail in a stone boat, you must have Faith.
But, with a cargo of Affection,
which Duns Scotus would call Love,
there is no cause for alarm.

For Bonnie Rideout

This is a stone boat.
Her name is Bonnie
and her cargo is Beauty,
which Plotinus would call Love.

She sails across wide seas and
wherever she is needed
there she sails, though
wounded by many storms.
Often she must jettison her cargo,
scattering Beauty all over the ocean,
yet, if you look into her bilges,
where other boats harbour drowned rats and diesel oil,
you will still find Beauty.

It is not known whether she gathers it to her
from the rain and wind on her marble and agate sails,
or whether she makes Beauty herself
in the darkest parts of her hull, where you can hear
the sound of the water against her keel
or selchies scratching their backs.

If you wish to journey in this stone boat,
you must be courageous, but
with a cargo of Beauty,
which Plotinus would call Love,
you should be able to face
the most tremendous seas.

For Barbara Purser

This is a stone boat.
Her name is Barbara
and her cargo is Memory,
which Saint Augustine would call Love.

So, whenever she anchors abroad,
she is always welcomed,
always offered a berth.

Often she leaves
whole cargoes of good Memories
laid out on cobbled quaysides,
for any who wish
to treasure, but

although she carries no guns
and waves no cutlasses,
pirates (who have very long memories)
fear her, for she is as swift and strong
as a cutter; can be sailed by one person alone;
and is intrepid in all weathers.

Being made of green marble from Connemara
with sails of the same stuff,
she is tinged with the green of the sea
and Memories of the land,
to both of which she is ever loyal.
She is rare, even among stone boats,
for her gunwales are green marble parallel lines
as beautiful as purfling on a cello.

If you wish to sail in this stone boat
you need to be True of Heart;
but, with a cargo of Memory,
which Saint Augustine would call Love,
you will receive treasures
beyond all pirate dreams.

Dedicatory Poems

For Sorley MacLean

You were the rowan tree at every gate.

To His Family in Memory of William Angel

What small thing has gone to ground this day;
leaf, rabbit, shrew or blackbird, pressed to clay
at the field's edge where the long clamps of straw
preserve the root crops by the graveyard wall,
each of its kind forgotten?
                              But let this memorial
recall for him your gentle thought; to spread
a leaf and feel its veins, or tuck the head
of a hurt blackbird close under your jaw
as though under a wing, or let a shrew
run from the rubbish right over your shoe
quite unmolested, or to help once more
the rabbit find its burrow from the gun –
for such as these could not have killed your son.

For Professor Doctor Ellen Hickmann

Honorary President of the International Study Group of Music Archaeology.

The clear clean stream of your thought flows from Michaelstein.
There is not a continent in which its quality is not known
and few are the countries ignorant of its virtues.

In the far Americas its quiet strength is felt in broad waters:
it mingles with the melting snows of the Andes:
it is honoured in India: it has touched the lips of Australia:

and in the lands of the Celts
the salmon of wisdom leaps delighted from its pool
knowing again from the clear stream of your thought
the taste of Truth.

For Maria Papageorgiou

Farmer and Tourist Guide

Proud you are, and with good cause for pride in this,
your homeland, where even the unnamed guest is honoured.

Stately and fine, you are an olive tree, forever young,
drawing rich stories from the soils of Greece.

You, your own harvester, press
from the bitter fruits of history
green memories; and, with the salt of humour,
render palatable their ancient animosities.

Devoted you are, but with wide open eyes
the bright intelligence of Athene's eyes –
you see far beyond folly to our shared humanity,
still worthy to preserve.

We, who have come to you anonymous and leave
sharing our names, call for no cauldrons,
seek no beaten gold; for you have filled
the old flasks of our minds with a rare vintage
and to your mountain gods you have been true.

*Note: In Homeric Greece the chief guests would be given parting gifts of
a cauldron, gold, or wine.*

For Martin Dalby

The delichon dalbica is a gentle bird
shy
modest
few have seen it
preening on the perch
but they have heard
more than a gentle trilling
or mild alarm call
from its secret
singing post
indeed its velvet viola
its kindly consort of strings
are prelude to

brash bands
songs its mother
never taught it
whole symphonies of sound
crashing upon the coasts
in extravagant waves

– as they withdraw
we find cast up
upon the shores
of hearing
a mary bean
Molucca mascot
warm and sensual
hold it in your palm
smell
the spice islands
hear
the sweet sung sentences
of love.

Note. "The Mary Bean" is the title of one of Martin's compositions and refers to Molucca beans which cross the Atlantic and are found on the shores of the Hebrides. Martin is a bird-watcher and a pilot. His true name is therefore Delichon Dalbica.

For Franco Staffa

High on the cliff
a silhouette betrays
the probing head
stretched neck
against a dusky sky.

My aim steady,
a single shot
drops him to a rock
out in the surge
of sea. The swell
gathers him.

I wade out to my waist –
the kilt floats, spreads
a tartan flower,
blue pleats petals
on winter waves –
and snatch his
trailing wing
on a receding tide.

Dripping up the steep
disused track,
the dead bird, hanging
upside-down,
its knuckled feet
in my fist's knuckled grip,
stretches its black wings
in a rising wind and
at the top,
catching the buffets of the air,
attempts another flight.

Homage to Jack Yeats

The light, half indigo half white:
bog asphodel, delicate tormentil,
hinted in heather shadows

a glint of peat-stained water, and the glow
of pale bog-cotton tufts:
soon, a short cool breeze, and dawn.

The man, half-raised,
with gentle summons
extends an arm
crooked at the elbow, wrist curved, palm
cupped to receive and give
due homage:

the white horse
alert from its own wanderings
tosses a willful head
acknowledging their bond
though his unwinking eyes
see other and beyond.

The man has slept no more
than needful, tall boots
still on.
          Who knows
what strange salvation
travels by horse and man
through ignorant lands,
their needs un-thought of,
sufferings un-bought.

But they have fodder:
from those secret hours,
alone, cool, passionate,
comes an old knowing
that will hold their fancies
through the hot stumbling

of a dusty road,
whose fiery angels, book and vial
– all the prophetic threats –
will be of little consequence
to the white horse, the shadow man:
for they have seen before the dawn and,
in the long day-span
of the north summer light,
know, now and forever,
there is no night.

In Memory of Mainie Jellett

You died the year that I was born
and so I claim no more than kinship;
yet this sketch in oils – some corn-stooks,
sea, the hills, the shallow glow
of threatened sunlight sixty years
ago: I saw these only yesterday
in this same place; the sheaves
(still sheaves) still gathered in by hand
and fed entire to the beasts – this sketch
brings you alive, perhaps as you were then,
intense as that blue band of sea.
Were your tears then more salt,
or did your blood run wild and brackish
as the sea runs in the Hebrides,
and was this painting how you smoothed
such troubled waters?
                          Fresh on this board
and through your eye in mine
they glisten still.

A City Herald

High above the city roost its true rulers,
the weathercocks.

After a giddy night they greet the dawn
in glittering plumage, and address their minds
to kingly thoughts and matters philosophical.

Humanity is beneath them
and they see nothing above
that is not a part of their own kingdom.

But they are out-done.
A top-floor tenement boy with a cheap telescope
also closes his night watch

and now, stravaiging through the square
with cockerel crow,
he passes people by
but, in his mind's eye, sees
the starlight pulsing
far beyond the sun.

For Katherine and Elliot Forbes on Their Final Move to the Banks of The Charles River

At the closing of the door leave no regrets:
slacken the guy-ropes, tug out rooted pegs,
strap up the costume cases, buckle to
the basketsful of properties, cease pacing
those fine floor-boards, passing by
elegant picture-lined arched passages:
the pad and shuffle of slippers is not your bequest
to this old house; you will have left
more generous echoes – and yourselves,
though seeking narrower spaces, will remain
forever uncontained; your talisman
that noble cream horse with his foreleg raised –
though cased in glass, still inching forward
through millennia ready to pace
new ramparts in defence of our first freedoms –
while you, worthy custodians,
will look abroad with equanimity
on the unreasoning river, knowing that where it goes
is where city to nature, body to spirit flows.

For Hinewirangi Kohu

Your blood is the clear sap
from the roots of the earth's garden:
your voice is heard singing
like the triumphant cry of a child
calling the blood-line from the womb -
tell me, how are such energies sustained?

I hear you answer – by the same life that lives
in all things, knowing the firefly
sparks bright against the moon
and that stars sing in the voice of one small bird –

But with such unequivocal magnificence
who will forgive you if, for one instant,
you should slip from grace, if not yourself?
and where are your private griefs assuaged?
who meets your longings with a radiant smile
to match your own in generosity?

So, to you, my Celtic Maori Queen,
I offer this small plant of poetry:
look! from my heart I hold it out to you:
I have placed
the gentlest of my kisses on its flower.

For Sir Iain Noble, 8.1.2010

This is the second time I've carried you.
The first was long ago, taking you from the boat
to land at Camus Fhionnairigh.

But now I cannot feel your chest
against my back, or my oar-chapped hands
hefting the undersides
of your tweed-clad thighs,
to keep you dryshod,
and save your fine brown brogues.
Ironic, that. Those fancy holes
recall a time when they were meant
to let the water in and out,
but no more so. Myself?
I was barefoot and happy in the sea,
my kilt clear of the waves,
my back proud of its burden.

You're heavier now, though you are shared
by six of us, and my bent leg is forced
into a limp – I wonder
are the middle pair bearing any weight?

At our backs, mid-winter sun
catches the snow on the summits
of those shapely mountain twins –
Beinn Sgritheall and Ladhar Bheinn.

Your summit now, good controversial friend,
is a small mound by your home,
with you, tucked up inside,
a peppermint in one pocket
and an agate heart alone
in a pocket on the other side.

One day its twin,
kept warm in her own pocket
by she who loves you still,
will join it and re-make the pair.

Meanwhile, may fairies attend you,
music and laughter. I am still happy
remembering that day
I took you through the sea,
but sad to say, there's no chance now
you'll carry me.

Poets in Kelvingrove Art Gallery

I lean over the stone balcony
looking down on friends from long ago:
on Eddie Morgan signing tirelessly:
Jack Rillie, my old tutor, biting a biscuit,
his daughter by his side; they are managing
his memory: Liz Lochhead, smiling
copiously, and professor Alan Riach
red-headed, taking it all in;
his parents, with their inlaid walking-sticks,
passing across the chequered floor.

It is as though these dear acquaintances are now
exhibits in the gallery of my thoughts;
as though the naked marble girl
beside my side, so frank and beautiful,
might gracefully descend the stairway
and walk with them –
or the stuffed birds and animals take flight,
and with them all the poets,
dipping pen feathers in sky blue,
wing their way westward, calling different calls,
and I be left unnoticed
in the glass case isolation of my mind.

Old Photograph

I know this old guitar to which he sings,
his eyebrows raised as though he sought
some unrequited Caribbean love.

I know his voice too, and the
exhalation and intake of his breath,
still steady on the beat, his pitching
perfect, undisturbed by chatter round about.

His the long-sighted gaze
of one who knew the sea,
envisaging beyond the ocean's edge
the land of his forefathers -
the purple haze of Scotland's summer hills.

Is that a whisper of a smile
between the syllables he sings,
his lips, just for this instant,
straightened and drawn thin?

These strings, as old as the guitar,
need nursing into tune -
and those two extra basses
only used at times
when memory plunges deep
into the darker pulses of the heart.

Sing on, old man. Your voice drifts pleasantly
across the rivers of death.

To Be Sung In Orbit

What if my sounds have no sound
but the slip of water on glass
or of threads spinning round
the spinner earth where they pass
beyond the hearing of all, what then?

Shall I ripple your view of the stars,
shout out defiance for long;
or cocoon the whole half-sleeping world
in a spinning song?

To the Library of Scottish Poetry

(The Canongate, The Royal Mile, Edinburgh*)

A nation is forged in the hearth

of poetry

* Lettering by John Creed. Commissioned by Richard Murphy Architects.

Lightning Source UK Ltd.
Milton Keynes UK
UKOW03f1111190914

238829UK00001B/8/P